Unstoppable

Living A Free And Fearless Life

Dr. Stem Sithembile Mahlatini.

Unstoppable

Living A Free And Fearless Life

Copyright © 2018 Dr. Stem Sithembile Mahlatini.
All rights reserved.

ISBN 978-1-7328275-8-5

All rights reserved. No part of this publication may be reproduced, stored in a retrieval system, or transmitted in any way by any means – electronic, mechanical, photocopy, recording, or otherwise – without the prior permissions of the copyright holder, except by reviewer who may quote brief passages in a review to be printed in magazine newspaper or by radio / TV announcement, as provided by USA copyright law. The author and the publisher will not be held responsible for any errors within the manuscript. All characters appearing in this work are fictitious. Any resemblance to real persons, living or dead is purely coincidental.

Written by: Dr. Stem Sithembile Mahlatini
Drstem14@gmail.com | www.drstemspeaks.com
https://www.drstemmie.com/
Facebook: DrStem Mahlatini Twitter: DrStemahlatini
LinkedIn: Drstem Mahlatini Skype: Dr.Mahlatini

Foreword by: Dr.Stem Sithembile Mahlatini Cover Design by: Masimba Mukundinashe Photo: Ted Hollins
https://tedhollins.photoreflect.com/
(407) 399-3664

Category: Historical, Biographical, Motivational, Inspirational, Educational and Empowerment
Library of Congress Cataloging-in-Publication Data **Printed in the USA**

Living A Free And Fearless Life

Foreword

This Life of Mine, I'm Gonna Make it Shine, Make it Shine, Make it Shine!!!

On Oct 24, 2018, I conjured the courage to go bald. Yes, I cut all my hair and decided to be Free and Fearless. A lot of people asked why? Some wondered why, but I knew that this bald move was unexplainable. However, I know why. I was tired of just talking and not moving my life and my work to the next level.

I was tired of emotional holds, excuses, unexplained fears, and family values. I was tired!

I also had looked at the calendar and realized we only had two months to the end of 2018, and that was not settling well with me. I needed to promise myself that 2019 was not going to be another stagnant year filled with empty promises, wishes, and a bucket full of plans.

I truly have to be thankful as I have also done well, since moving to Orlando, FL from Boston in 2016. It was a very, very rough start. I was diagnosed with Diabetes and High Blood Pressure a month after I arrived in Orlando. My sugars were 520 which unbeknownst to me was close to a diabetic coma. The Lord was gracious to save me as I would have died Sept 25, 2016 in my sleep. My gratitude to my family, friends Rhonda and Christopher Soudart who came to the rescue and provided me accommodation, mental and emotional support until I got back on my feet.

I also had a very rare opportunity to work at the Orange County Library as the first social worker in the Library in the whole state of Florida. My gratitude to Sara Brown Benjamin and Donna Bachowski who were my bosses.

They took care of me in my most vulnerable time and offered me support and supervision to help me serve the homeless population that came into the library seeking assistance.

We are all a paycheck away from being homeless. This I learned the hard way. By the way, save your money. Be careful not to be a secret angel to those who love you when you have money, save your money. They will not be anywhere near helping you when you are down.

Being bald has brought me to another level of baldness. I will now take even bigger risks and take my life to a level higher than I've ever dreamt. I now know being bald means change. Change is not easy. It is true you cannot expect to get different results being in the same place, doing the same things. You will have to change to get different results.

It isn't easy to make changes, but there's no better advice than this: just do your best. Make sure you stay strong enough to move ahead, because there are some wonderful rewards waiting for you when you get the courage to be bald. Not every change you will make will makes sense right away, but with time, you will definitely start to see answers, decisions will prove to be the right ones, and the path will become clearer.

Giving up has never been an option for me. I always tell people that my biggest risk was leaving my parents and siblings in Zimbabwe and embarking to the USA in 1986. After that, every other move and risk had to be taken to live the free and fearless life I came to seek.

My dream is to have enough money to go back and help those in Zimbabwe, build schools, hospitals, training schools and help those that want to start businesses or go to college. To do that, I have to have money, and to have money, I have to take even bigger risks.

In my language shona we have this saying, " Shungu dzarwizi". Ask me in my live workshops to explain, because I will be meeting you soon, if you are reading this. We will absolutely meet and talk about your journey and my journey in one of my workshops.

For three years since moving to Orlando, FL, I honestly thought I could never regain my energy, zeal and excitement of becoming the world renounced motivational speaker, workshop presenter, retreat coordinator, television and radio personality I have always wanted to be. But, today, I am digging my dusty dreams out of my own fears, known and unknown.

My vivid, complicated, detailed dreams are back. The running dialogue in my head as I live my life has returned. The big dreamer is dreaming big and acting boldly again. And, I must say, it feels really good!

I know that I have the courage to be fearless. Will you follow along? When my confidence wavers, when I start to mumble, will you remind me fear is a measly four-letter word? Enjoy this guide to becoming a free and fearless you.

This book is a sign of my rebirth. It is the result of my new baldness and boldness. It is my way to help you become your best, as well. I know without a shadow of doubt that whatever I have been able to do, you can do it too, and more. I also know that what others have done, I too can do.

To my parents, Benjamin and Idah Mahlatini, thank you for giving me life. My siblings, nieces and nephews, I can only be and do the best me to lead you. Be your best and everything will work out. To all my supporters, followers and prayer warriors, may God open up doors for you like never before. Be Encouraged and Encouraging.

After reading this book, I look forward to hearing your story and how you were able to boldly make decisions that have changed your life for the better by living fearlessly and free.

Email me at drstem14@gmail.com

If you would like me to interview you on my radio show The DrStem Show:
https://americaoutloud.com/show/the-drstem-show/

Email me at drstem@americaoutloud.com

You've Only got three choices in life: Give Up, Give in or Give it all you've got.

Contents

1. **Know Who You Are:** Understanding Your Personality And Identity..................13

2. **Having The Right Attitude:** Being Positive..................39

3. Know Your Purpose and What You Want In Life......59

4. Self Worth..................67

5. Self-Efficiacy and Self-Confidence..................73

6. Vision And Goals..................83

7. Emotional Competence..................89

8. **Emotional Strongholds:** Overcoming Doubt and More..................93

9. **Developing A Fearless Mindset:** What It Means To Be Bold And Fearless.................. 105

10. **Dealing With failure:** Starting Over..................111

11. Listening And Effective Communication:.................. 123

12. The Freedom Of Forgiveness.................. 133

13. Patience..................139

14. Gratitude..................147

15. Helping Others To Succeed.................. 159

16. Creating A Life Of Success..................165

17. Celebrating Small Success... 183

18. Love, Laugh And Live:... 191

19. Hope, Peace & Joy.. 197

Appendix:

i. Motivational Quotes:... 204

ii. It's Time To Fly: 208

ii. Epilogue: 211

ii. Let's Connect:.. 215

ii. About The Author.:.. 222

"The only person you are destined to become is the person you decide to be.

Ralph Waldo Emerson

"It's your place in the world; it's your life. Go on and do all you can with it, and make it the life you want to live. ".

Mae Jemison

Dr.**Stem**

Unstoppable

Living A Free And Fearless Life

Know Who You Are: Understanding Your Personality And Identity

Congratulations! If you're reading this book, it means you're ready for change--something different, something new, a fresh start. You recognize there's something inside of you that needs to be birthed. You might not understand when or how but you know what it is and you simply need the courage to do it. If this is you, you've come to the right place.

Upon completing this book, you will have gained tools and concepts that will allow you to be fearless so that you can excel in whatever it is you want to set out to do in life. But, before we jump right into how to become unstoppable, let's explore a little about you.

What type of person are you? Are you an introvert--do you like to keep to yourself and shy away from others, or are you an extrovert who enjoys socializing and being around other people?

Do you readily speak your mind, or are you more reserved in your thoughts? Are you a "go-getter" who jumps at any opportunity for success, or are you more practical in nature in that you like to take your time and weigh your options? Do you like to take chances, or do you like to invest your time and money in things that are "tried and true"? These are all very important questions that every person striving for success in life should ask themselves.

Why? Because your identity and thought-processes will determine your actions. Your actions are a reflection of who you are and how you think.

How you perceive the world around you also plays a huge part in how you identify with the world. For example, if you think the world has no good in it and everyone's out to get you, you'll likely approach everything you do with this mindset--apprehensive, non-trusting, skeptical.

On the other hand, if you see the world as a place full of opportunity and filled with hope, you're more likely to approach life with the attitude that anything is possible. You're also likely to be more trusting and optimistic about the things you want to achieve in life.

There's no right or wrong personality. In fact, there are pros and cons to both. What's most important is that you recognize the attributes of your personality and how you identify with yourself and the world around you. Doing so will bring you a sense of personal awareness that allows you to achieve balance.

For example, being aware of how you assert yourself can inform your approach to your life goals and with the people you encounter throughout your journey.

You are who you are by nature, but there are certainly things that influence who we are, such as life experiences, background, culture, family members, friends, and even our religious and political views.

It's important that regardless of your views, you nurture the positive aspects of your personality and strive to work on weaknesses. Being fearless will require you to know exactly who you are and what your strengths and weaknesses are.

*"Believe in yourself and all that you are.
Know that there is something inside you
that is greater than any obstacle".*

– Christian D. Larson

Self- Reflection
Know Who You are: Understanding Your Personality And Identity

Understanding Your Personality and Identity

"To know thyself is the beginning of wisdom" This famous quote is often attributed to Socrates. But what exactly do you know when you "know yourself?"

The Benefits of Self-Knowledge

In the past 20 years, I have worked with people of all nationalities who were seeking counseling, life and career coaching. If I can summarize all the work I have done and continue to do in two words, they would be "Know Thyself". Here are a few reasons why you might want to know yourself:

Happiness. You will be happier when you can express who you are. Expressing your desires, moreover, holds you accountable for saying what you want increased the likelihood of you getting what you want.

Less inner conflict. When your outside actions are in agreement with your inner feelings and values, you will experience less inner conflict, low self-worth, misery, anger, insecurity and resentment.

Better decision-making. When you know yourself, you are able to make better choices about everything, from small decisions like which sweater you'll buy to big decisions like which partner you'll spend your life with. Knowing yourself is a compass for what you will and won't tolerate. You'll have Knowing yourself helps you to establish guidelines you can apply to solve life's various problems. When it comes to your life, you become and no-nonsense person who knows what they want, "Yes" is "Yes" and "No" is "No".

Self-Control. When you know yourself, you understand what motivates you to resist bad habits and develop good ones. You'll have the insight to know which values and goals activate your willpower. You listen to that small voice, that nudge that speaks to you, makes you excited or anxious. If it does not feel good, always, take some time to evaluate before moving forward with your decision.

Resistance to social pressure. As I mentioned prior, when you know yourself, you are grounded in your values and preferences, so it is easier to say "yes" when you want to say "Yes" and "No when you mean "No." Many people are unfulfilled because they believe they will find happiness based on what's trending or the experiences and opinions of those around them. However, the experiences that lead to your fulfillment can only be achieved by you understanding what works for you, not the social trends and expectations surrounding you.

Tolerance and Understanding of others. Your awareness of your own weaknesses and struggles can help you understand others. This level of understanding also helps you to empathize with others and extend your patience. Tolerance and understanding can improve your relationship with others dramatically.

Vitality and pleasure: Being who you truly are helps you feel more alive and makes your experience of life richer, larger, and more exciting. This is because you're not weighed down by other people's expectations of you or unrealistic expectations you once had of yourself. Being free makes you feel alive. When you feel alive, the glass is always half full, or running over!

THE BUILDING BLOCKS OF KNOWING THYSELF

Building Block 1: Understanding Your Values

"Values"—such as "helping others," "being creative," health, "financial security," and so on—are what helps you make decisions and choices in life. Values can also keep you going even when you are tired. They make you push yourself when you feel you can't do anymore. This is because you have something within you that you are committed to holding true to.

Values also serve as accountability measures. Without them, there would be nothing to remind you to do the right thing or be the best that you could be.

What are your values?

If you want to self-motivate, know your values. Here are examples of personal values:

- **Love** - patience, kindness, forgiveness, trust, selflessness, compassion and protection.

- **Integrity** - honesty, truthfulness, responsibility, reliability, dependability, consistency, decency, justice, sincerity and commitment

- **Stewardship** - resourcefulness, charity, contribution, or giving.

- **Wisdom** - intelligence, understanding, knowledge, good judgment, insight, perception, discipline, experience, personal growth, discretion and intuition.

- **Freedom** - independence, free will, liberty, autonomy, and/or self-determination.

- **Achievement** - success, or accomplishment

- **Happiness** - joy, contentment, pleasure, bliss, delight, and/or gladness

- **Peace** - harmony, unity, tranquility, or serenity.

- **Perseverance** - persistence, or determination.

- **Respect** - appreciate, esteem, value, or cherish

Building Block 2: Interests

Knowing Thyself means knowing your Interests. "Interests" include your passions, hobbies, and anything that draws your attention, mind, spirit and body, over a sustained period of time. To figure out your interests, ask yourself these questions:

What do you pay attention to? What are you curious about? What concerns you? Take time to quiet your mind, meditate, sit in silence and relax so that you achieve focused answers.

Knowing thyself makes life vivid and may give you clues to your deepest passions. Now, that's exciting! Many people have built a career around a deep interest in something. For example, my career has been built around my passion.

My passion is built around my excitement when people get their "Aha" moments, stop sweating the small stuff and begin living their best life, shamelessly and effortlessly.

Building Block 3: Temperament

Knowing thyself means managing your temperament. "Temperament" describes your inborn preferences. Do you restore your energy from being alone 'Introvert" or from being with people 'extrovert'? Are you a planner or go-with-the-flow type of person? Do you make decisions more on the basis of feelings, deep thought or facts?

Do you prefer details or "Big Ideas"? Knowing the answers to temperament questions like these could help you gravitate toward situations, people, places in which you could flourish, and avoid situations in which you could fade away slowly.

Building Block 4: Being The Real You

Are you a morning person or a night person, for example? At what time of day does your energy peak?

If you schedule activities when you are at your best, you are respecting your inborn biology. As I look back on my life, I realize I've been a morning person since birth. I wake up at 5am with no alarm, and by the time everyone is struggling to get in the office at 8 or 9 am, I am on my lunch break (figuratively). I am that personwho, when you walk into my office in the morning greets you with a hyper, happy, nothing bothers me, " hello" or 'good morning" attitude . I am a morning person in all aspects.

What is your preference? Are you with a significant other you complement and who compliments you in bringing out the best in you? Figure out your preferences and start following your heart. You will be amazed at the energy you have if you respect your inborn biology, whether it's in the evening or in the morning, like me.

Building Block 5: Your life Mission

You cannot bypass this building block, even if you wanted to. It is that critical to becoming an unstoppable, free and fearless person. Creating a life mission to me is like creating the address where you want to be in life. It is the address to your life GPS, which directs all of your wants and needs.

To begin answer the following question: *"What have been the most meaningful events of your life?"*

I answered this question when I wrote the book, "It's Time to shift – From Fear to Faith". I realized at that time that my most meaningful and rewarding moment had been my work as a nursing assistant in a nursing home in Lowell Mass. I realized that caring for people at the end of life when they are no longer able to care for themselves gave me joy and fulfillment.

I eventually realized that talking to elderly, young and everyone in the middle gave me even more joy and meaning because I enjoy talking to and helping people. I find it rewarding to help others process and find resolve, which helps them to overcome their past and plan for the future.

It is an exciting opportunity to bring light to someone who has been feeling down and in the dark. It brings me joy to see the light in someone's eyes when they decide to make their joy, peace and happiness number one.

It is my mission. I have been able to reach hundreds of thousands through my speaking engagements, workshops, seminars, conferences, books, in office and telephone counseling and coaching, television and radio.

Ask yourself the same question: *"What have been the most meaningful events of my life?"*

You may discover clues to your hidden identity, to your career, and to life satisfaction.

Building Block 6: Strengths

Knowing your strengths is one of the foundations of knowing thyself. "Strengths" can include not only abilities, skills, and talents, but also character strengths such as loyalty, respect for others, love for learning, emotional intelligence, fairness, and more.

Not being able to acknowledge your own superpowers could put you on the path to low-self-esteem, low self-worth and inability to live your best unstoppable, free and fearless life. You will benefit from becoming a person who "takes in the good," listening for compliments and noticing skills that could be clues to your strengths.

Many people are provided with positive feedback about what their good qualities are, but do nothing with the information. You will need to break that cycle if you are to become Unstoppable. Strive to do something about the talents, strengths that are pointed out to you. Your talents will never be fully realized unless you nurture them.

Know your strengths. I had a beautiful soul come to my office and she tearfully shared with me what she has been told since she was young, that she has a soulful soothing voice. I immediately asked her to sing my favorite song ever "Amazing Grace".

We both were teary eyed when she sang it. It was amazing. What she has done with that voice, only God knows. I hope she is doing something with it. What I do know is that she was willing to nurture her talent in that moment by sharing one of her best qualities with me.

What would you do with that knowledge of what your best qualities and weaknesses are? Likewise, knowing your weaknesses can also help you be honest with yourself (or others) about what you are NOT so good at.

You might decide either to work on those weaknesses or try to make them a smaller part of your personal or career life. It is all up to you, what you choose to do. Being aware of what your strengths and weaknesses are can certainly help to guide your choice.

Building Block 7: Being True to You

Even if you know the building blocks and purpose to practice them, it's hard to remain true to yourself because you are constantly changing and life happens. Society's values often conflict with your own, but remember, you are in control of you. It would be a shame spend the majority of your life living out other people's vision for you, only to one day realize you don't have much time to do the things you want to do. Yes, you are growing older. Being true to yourself also means not ever having to regret being a good person to the wrong people.

You understand that your behavior says everything about you, and other people's behavior says everything about them. You understand that we are all different, and you will not be able to change anyone. At best, you can meet them half-way so that you achieve a 'win-win' for everyone in every situation.

"My first commandment is to "Be Stem (Sithembile)"—My mission is to be so busy loving my life, my being here that I have no time for hate, regret, worry, fret or fear. Helping others find their true self is my calling. For all of us, being yourself sounds easier than it actually is! It takes work. However, it is a journey worth every step.

Now you are ready to answer the following question.

Δ Who are you? What about your identity and personality informs your purpose?

_____

_____

_____

_____

_____

_____

YOUR STRENGTHS & WEAKNESSES

Your strengths are things you can leverage on, things you can use to push yourself further. On the other hand, your weaknesses are not your downfall. These are areas you need to improve on. It is not something you lack. It is something you need to develop and build.

It's not unusual for people to compare themselves with others around them, and to feel superior or inferior towards them based on their strengths and their weaknesses.

The thing is, every individual is different, and we all function differently based on our personalities. It is important to know yourself and your capacities.
In order to leverage your strengths and improve on your weaknesses, you first need to know them.

Knowing your personal strengths

Your biggest personal strength would be something that comes very easily for you. Take some time and think about what comes naturally for you. It could be anything.

Examples of Personal Strengths

- Accuracy
- ACTION oriented
- adventurous
- ambitious
- Analytical
- appreciative
- artistic
- athletic
- authentic
- caring
- clever
- compassionate
- charm
- communicative
- confident
- considerate
- courage
- creativity
- critical thinking
- curiosity
- dedication
- determination
- discipline
- educated
- empathetic
- energetic
- entertaining
- enthusiastic
- fair
- fast
- flexible
- focused
- forceful
- friendliness
- generosity
- gratitude
- helpfulness
- honesty
- Hope
- humility
- humor
- idealism
- Independence
- ingenuity
- industriousness
- inner Peace
- inspirational
- integrity
- intelligence
- kindness

- knowledgeable
- leadership
- lively
- logical
- love
- love of learning
- mercy
- modesty
- motivation
- observant
- optimistic
- open minded
- orderly
- originality
- organization
- outgoing
- patient
- perseverance
- persuasiveness
- persistence
- practical
- precise
- problem solving
- Prudence
- respect
- responsibility
- self assurance
- seriousness
- self control
- spirituality
- spontaneous
- social intelligence
- social skills
- straightforward
- strategic thinking
- tactful
- team oriented
- thoughtful
- thrifty
- tolerant
- trustworthy
- versatile
- visionary
- vitality
- warmth
- willpower
- wisdom

General Strengths in the Workplace

- adapting
- administering
- analyzing
- arranging
- advising
- budgeting
- building teams
- briefing
- balancing
- communicating
- controlling
- coordinating
- creating
- checking
- counseling
- compiling
- coaching
- deciding
- detailing
- developing people
- directing
- devising
- discovering
- data input
- empathizing
- evaluating
- examining
- explaining
- editing
- empowering
- fixing
- formulating
- finalizing
- guiding a group or an individual
- gathering information
- generating ideas
- giving feedback
- helping
- handling
- hosting
- imagining
- implementing
- influencing
- initiating
- innovating
- interviewing
- instructing
- judging
- learning

- listening
- locating
- launching
- leading
- managing
- mentoring
- monitoring
- motivating
- marketing
- negotiating
- navigating
- observing
- organizing
- overhauling
- overseeing
- persuading
- planning
- preparing
- presenting
- problem-solving
- proofreading
- prioritizing
- questioning
- qualifying
- researching
- resolving
- reporting
- recording
- repairing
- reviewing
- scheduling
- selling
- supervising
- simplifying
- speaking
- strategizing
- teaching
- team-working
- troubleshooting
- training
- tracking details
- thinking creatively
- understanding
- uniting
- upgrading
- updating
- verbalizing
- volunteering
- verifying
- writing

GENERAL STRENGTHS OF LEADERS AND MANAGERS

Communication Strengths
- clear and concise in verbalizing ideas
- allow effective communication
- able to summarize and clarify
- actively listen to ideas
- give constructive criticism
- take time to make a personal connection

Strengths for Providing Direction
- make objectives and outcomes specific
- clearly communicate objectives and outcomes
- able to fully explain tasks and delegate them
- create and provide clear standards and expectations
- develop checks and controls
- oversee staff to keep them on task

Strengths for Supporting Staff
- know talents of workers in order to delegate effectively
- provide staff training and development
- empower workers by delegating some responsibilities
- evaluate staff performance on a regular basis
- recognize efforts of workers
- support staff to increase efficiency

Strengths for Decision Making & Judgment
- clearly define and communicate issues
- gather important information
- make decisions on the best ACTION to take
- implements the course of ACTION
- communicate and explain decisions
- follow up on progress of ACTION
- learn from previous mistakes

Organizing and Planning Strengths
- define concrete goals
- explain goals in detail
- create a plan to achieve goals
- gather and assign resources
- motive the staff for highest level of performance
- evaluate progress and provide feedback

Problem Solving Strengths
- recognize the problem
- analyze the relevant information
- understand cause and effect relationships
- develop possible solutions
- choose the best solution and implement it

Examples of Weaknesses

- Not taking criticism well
- Impatient
- Lazy
- Easily bored
- Procrastinate
- Persistent
- Takes things personally
- Strong willed
- Passive
- Does not like conflict
- Shy
- Lethargic
- Long-term planning
- Strict
- Short-sighted
- Selfish
- Focusing on small details
- Takes blame for others
- Being straight forward
- Greedy
- Delegating tasks
- Needs to be right
- Stubborn
- Multitasking
- Allows emotions to show
- Blunt
- Presenting
- Impulsive
- Bossy
- Takes on to much
- Follow-ups
- Aggressive
- Likes to take risks
- Critical of others
- Passive
- Works to much
- Perfectionist
- Fearful
- Self critic
- Trouble with teams
- Close-minded
- Unorganized
- Does not like pressure

Using the lists of strengths and weaknesses I have given you, answer the following question. Use separate journal to answer these questions so that you do not limit yourself. Write as much as you can to get a better understanding of your own personal weaknesses and strengths.

Δ What are some strengths and weaknesses of your personality that you need to be mindful of?

_____
_____
_____
_____
_____
_____
_____
_____
_____
_____
_____
_____

PESSIMISTIC VS OPTIMISTIC

People are typically put into one of two categories. They're either optimistic or pessimistic. Your optimism or pessimism shapes your world view. You see the glass as half empty or half full, and that is how you describe your position in life.

When people are too optimistic or too pessimistic, they live outside of reality.

You want to be somewhere in the middle. You want to have a nice dose of optimism, but you want to have your feet on the ground at the same time. The difference is all in how people choose to live their life one moment at a time.

Optimist

The dictionary describes an optimist as follows: A person who tends to be hopeful and confident about the future or the success of something. A person who believes that this world is the best of all possible worlds or that good must ultimately prevail over evil.

Pessimist

The dictionary describes a pessimist as follows: a person who tends to see the worst aspect of things or believe that the worst will happen. A person who believes that this world is as bad as it could be or that evil will ultimately prevail over good.

Pessimistic people think of the worst. They have the tendency to expect the worst in everything. When they are in a relationship, they are the one sure that there must be something wrong with the person they are in love with.

Optimism Phrases
Here ARE examples of optimism sayings and popular phrases to help you better understand optimism.

- seeing the Glass half full instead of half empty.
- when life hands you lemons, make lemonade.
- every cloud has a silver lining.
- Hope against Hope.
- things have a way of working out for the best.
- there is light at the end of the tunnel.
- keep your chin up.
- hang in there.
- there ARE plenty of Fish in the sea.
- when one door closes, another one opens.
- see the world through rose-colored glasses.
- count your blessings.
- everything is coming up roses.

Pessimism
Pessimism is having an attitude of hopelessness toward life and toward existence, coupled with a vague general opinion

that pain and evil outweigh everything. Pessimism is the opposite of optimism, an attitude of general hopefulness, coupled with the view that there is a balance of good and pleasure in the world.

You Can Change

People say that you're born an optimist or a pessimist, but I believe people can change. You are not stuck as an optimist or a pessimist. With help and guidance, you can be who you want to be.

∆ Do you find yourself being more optimistic or pessimistic about things? Why? How does this help or hinder you?

_____

_____

_____

_____

_____

_____

_____

Having The Right Attitude: Being Positive

You must have the right attitude if you're going to live fearlessly. In fact, having the wrong attitude will make you easily stoppable. So, what is the right attitude? It's one that is positive and optimistic. This doesn't mean that you'll never be skeptical of anything. It simply means that you won't allow your skepticism to overshadow your ability to be optimistic.

Fear feeds on distrust and disbelief and wreaks havoc on your attitude. This also holds true for the attitude you have about yourself and toward others. If you do not have respect for yourself or those around you, you'll only distance yourself further from your goals.

Rather than being fearless, you'll find that you've become just the opposite--fearful, unproductive, stagnant and, worst of all, unpleasant to be around. Surround yourself with people and things that are positive--things that motivate you, inspire you and push you to be the best version of yourself. Anything that is counterproductive to being positive should not be the focus of your time and energy. Unfortunately, this includes people. It can be especially hard for us to distance ourselves from friends or loved ones because of their negative influences. But, once you know who you are and what you're after, distancing yourself from these negative influences becomes much easier, and so will maintaining a positive attitude.

Having the right attitude often drives people to productivity through their words and actions. It connects you with others who have similar attitudes about life and often opens doors. It serves as fuel for your life journey and puts fear in its place--the back seat.

"Of course motivation is not permanent. But then, neither is bathing; but it is something you should do on a regular" basis.

-Zig Ziglar

Self- Reflection
Having The Right Attitude

THE POWER OF ATTITUDE

The reality and great news is that you determine your attitude. Your attitude is one of the few things in life over which you have TOTAL control. For better or worse, your attitude affects your performance. Your attitude has a profound impact on the way you interact or live with other people. It affects the way you fit in with different groups of people at work and home.

Your attitude has a direct impact on how you communicate and collaborate with others, how you contribute to the culture of your work environment, and how you perform your daily tasks and responsibilities. Ultimately, your attitude shapes your success and your happiness. Other things being equal, the person with the best attitude will win.

It is interesting when I do couples counseling how people's attitudes are the main indicator of why couples have communication problems that can be so deep.

Unfortunately, many people cling to beliefs and attitudes that restrict rather than encourage them to take a good look at their attitude and how it impact their day to day life and relationships.

Let me dive deeper into what attitude is, because I believe when you know better you do better.

What is Attitude?

Attitude is the way you look at life. It is the way you choose to see and respond to events, situations, people, and yourself. Your attitude is not something that happens to you. You choose your attitude. Your attitude is created by your thoughts, and you choose your thoughts.

- You are the architect of your frame of mind.
- You decide how you will perceive and process the events of life and work.
- You make the decision if your mindset is positive or negative.

If you want to feel better, you have to think better. In order to be positive in the way you feel, it is necessary to be disciplined in the way you think. Change begins within you. Your mind has enormous power. Indeed, your mind is your most important change resource. How you see and respond to the events of life and work is shaped by your mindset and patterns of thinking. It is all on you, not your parents' way of raising you, your circumstances or environment. It is your choice. Therefore, an essential key to becoming Unstoppable Free and Fearless is to train your mind and use it wisely.

Negative Attitude

A negative attitude is the result of negative thinking. It's not what happens to you that brings about a negative attitude, it is how you choose to react or respond to what has happened to you. It is how you choose to deal with the situation, or event. Negative attitude is a lack of mental discipline. It focuses on the problem rather than solutions or opportunities.

A negative attitude can only survive on a steady diet of negative thinking and negative self-talk. A negative attitude impacts you and the people around you in all aspects of your life. A negative attitude affects you negatively, physically, mentally, spiritually and emotionally. A person with a negative attitude will almost always lose to a person with a positive attitude.

Sadly, many people with a negative attitude are stuck in a cycle of negativity because they have a negative attitude about improving their attitude. This is not a good place to be! Good news is you have the power to change your thinking and how you choose to deal with life as a whole.

Positive Attitude

A positive attitude is the result of a disciplined and deliberate way of seeing, thinking, and responding to life. It is a mental discipline. It is intentional. It is mental toughness. A positive attitude is not naïve, and it does not sugarcoat problems. Rather, it sees and acknowledges problems and then focuses on finding solutions and opportunities.

It looks for the opportunity within the problem. A positive attitude attracts good from those around you. A positive attitude affects you positively, physically, mentally, spiritually and emotionally.

One of the most important steps you can take toward becoming unstoppable and achieving your greatest potential in life is to learn to monitor your attitude and its impact on your work performance, relationships and everyone around you. We all have a choice.

We can choose an inner dialogue of self-encouragement and self-motivation, or we can choose one of self-defeat, anger, resentment and self-pity. It's a power we all have.

Each of us encounters hard times, hurt feelings, heartache, and physical and emotional pain. The key is to realize it's not what happens to you that matters; it's how you choose to respond.

Did you know that your mind is a computer that can be programmed?

The best part is you can choose whether the software installed is productive or unproductive. Your inner dialogue is the software that programs your attitude, which determines how you present yourself to the world around you. You have control over the programming. Whatever you put into it is reflected in what comes out.

Many of us have behavior patterns today that were programmed into our brains at a very tender age. The information that was recorded by our brains could have been completely inaccurate, hurtful, painful or cruel. The sad reality of life is that we will continue to hear negative information, but we don't have to program it into our brains.

The loudest and most influential voice you hear is your own inner voice, your own self-critic. It can work for or against you, depending on the messages you allow. It can be optimistic or pessimistic (see the section on optimistic and pessimistic).

Self-critic voice can wear you down or cheer you on. You control the sender and the receiver, but only if you consciously, knowingly take responsibility for and control over your inner conversation. You can silence the self-critic or change the message at any given moment.

Negativity, anger, resentment and bad attitudes are often the product of past experiences and events. Common causes include low-self-esteem, low self-worth, rejection, violation, stress, fear, resentment, anger and an inability to handle change.

It takes serious work to examine the roots of a harmful attitude, but the rewards of ridding ourselves of this heavy baggage can last a lifetime.

Helping people rid this heavy burden and baggage is my life, so if you need guidance and support, I provide telephone, video or in person coaching sessions to help you get over the hump. You can also contact any local licensed professionals in your area to help you resolve these past hurts and memories.

Here are a few of the strategies I have used myself and shared with my clients in session or at workshops and seminars.

1. Using Affirmations

Affirmations are positive statements you say to yourself to keep you motivated, inspired, empowered to follow your heart and anticipate manifestation of all that you ask for. Affirmations repeated several times each day, every day, serve to reprogram your subconscious with positive thinking.

An affirmation is made up of words charged with power, conviction and faith. You send a positive response to your subconscious, which accepts whatever you tell it. When done properly, this triggers positive feelings that, in turn, drive action.

Examples of affirmations that I share with those I work with.

Self-confidence affirmations

- **I deserve to be happy and successful.**
- **I have the power to change myself.**
- **I can forgive and understand others and their motives.**
- **I can make my own choices and decisions.**

- I am free to choose to live as I wish and to give priority to my desires.

- I can choose happiness whenever I wish no matter what my circumstances

- I am flexible and open to change in every aspect of my life

- I act with confidence having a general plan and accept plans are open to alteration

- It is enough to have done my best

- I deserve to be loved

- I love meeting strangers and approach them with boldness and enthusiasm.

- I am self-reliant, creative and persistent in whatever I do.

- I love change and easily adjust myself to new situations.

- I always see only the good in others. I attract only positive people.

- When I breath, I inhale confidence and exhale timidity.

- I love meeting strangers and approach them with boldness and enthusiasm.

- I approve of myself and love myself deeply and completely.
- I live in the present and am confident of the future.
- My personality exudes confidence. I am bold and outgoing.
- I am self-reliant, creative and persistent in whatever I do.
- I am energetic and enthusiastic. Confidence is my second nature.
- I always attract only the best of circumstances and the best positive people in my life.
- I am a problem solver. I focus on solutions and always find the best solution.
- I love change and easily adjust myself to new situations.
- I love challenges. They bring out the best in me.
- I am well groomed, healthy and full of confidence.
- My outer well-being is matched by my inner well-being.
- Self confidence is what I thrive on.

- **Nothing is impossible and life is great.**
- **I always see only the good in others. I attract only positive people.**
- **I face difficult situations with courage and conviction. I always find a way out of such situations.**
- **Add More of Your Own**

2. Discovering what Motivates You

Until you discover what motivates you—what incites you, it will always be difficult or challenging to take the necessary action to change your life.

You will need motivation that includes: love, self-preservation, happiness, financial freedom, financial gain and a better life. Self-motivation requires enthusiasm, a positive outlook, a positive physiology (walk faster, smile, sit up), and a belief in yourself and your God-given potential.

You see things that all others cannot imagine or see. You feel good about where you are going and know without a shadow of doubt that all things are possible. No matter what, all your heart desires will come to pass.

3. Understanding the Power of Visualization

Nelson Mandela wrote extensively on how visualization helped him maintain a positive attitude while being imprisoned for 27 years. "I thought continually of the day when I would walk free.

I fantasized about what I would like to do," he wrote in his autobiography. *Visualization works.*

When you listen to all those people who have acquired wealth, health and desired dreams, they all talk about how they saw themselves doing what they are doing now or having what they have before it came to pass.

Studies have found that the greatest athletes, surgeons, engineers and artists use affirmations and visualizations either consciously or subconsciously, to enhance and focus their skills. I use visualization all the time. This book was visualized 5 years before I could finish and publish it.

Visualization works. Best way to do this is to put together a vision board that you can visualize at all times.

When you visualize you materialize

4. Dialogue Check

Your inner dialogue is key to changing your outlook, innerlook and overall attitude. Attitude talk is a way to heal the past hurts, situations, effects of what people have done or said about you that do not make you who you are or who you can be. Dialogue check is checking what you say to yourself, what you believe and how you see yourself. Dialogue check is making sure your internal conversation is one that is positive and helpful to you.

Your internal conversation—that little voice you listen to all day long—acts like a seed in that it programs your brain and affects your behavior. Do a dialogue check by taking a closer look at what you are saying to yourself.

5. Words Have Power

Once released to the universe, our words cannot be taken back. I once learned about this concept " WOW—watch our words". Did you know what we speak reflects what is already in our hearts based upon all the things we have come to believe about ourselves?

If we find ourselves speaking judgmentally, resentfully and disapprovingly about our circumstances or those around us, we know the condition of our hearts needs to change.

You can create a direct path to success by what you say and think. Words have power, change them if you have to. You have the power.

6. The Power in a Smile and Positive Greeting

There is an immense power found within a smile. A smile conveys feelings of happiness, hope and positivity to anyone who sees it. When you smile, you are sending a message to those around you that you are accepted, you are welcome, all is well. A smile indicates a positive attitude.

A smile on its own can change your inner dialogue it requires your inner feelings are also required to rise to the occasion of positivity. I am always smiling. Even when I am deep in thought and forget to smile to a stranger, I will say "smile". Can you imagine? This says a lot about who I am. I am one who is happy and smiling at all times. When I am in that zone, more people seem to enjoy being around me and feel comfortable being in my presence.

This is the reason I am always playing music to ensure I am in a happy smiley positive mind frame. Most people enjoy working and living with those who go out of their way to smile and bring the best out themselves and others. A smile has power and yes change your greeting to something powerful and cheerful.

If someone asks; "how are you," try, "I am fantabulous!"

Man Becomes what He Thinks About

7. Encouragement and Enthusiasm

Encouragement and Enthusiasm is staying motivated. Enthusiasm is to attitude what breathing is to life. Being enthusiastic allows you to apply your talents more effectively. You are excited, encouraged, empowered to commit yourself to your desires and dreams. It's an internal spirit that speaks through your actions from your commitment and your belief in what you are doing. Enthusiasm is one of the most empowering and attractive characteristics you can have.

If you have met me, you know how enthusiastic I am. I believe when God said look, child, I know the plans I have for you, plans to prosper you and not to harm or hurt you, he meant it. Who am I to doubt his plan? I will continue to trust and be enthusiastic about life. Will you?

8. Your Spirituality

There are four human needs we need to pay attention to at all times, physical, spiritual, mental and emotional. Just as we feed our bodies in response to our primary need to survive physically, we need to feed our spirit because we are spiritual beings. Many people find powerful and positive motivation in their faith. I happen to be one of them. How do you feed your spiritual realm?

9. Using Humor

Humor is a powerful motivator. The more humor and laughter in your life, the less stress you'll have, which means more positive energy to help you put your attitude into action. There are also health benefits to lightening up. Here are some of the health benefits to remind you to smile every moment you get. Laughter is the best medicine in many ways:

Humor neutralizes fear. Humor can crack through the ice and take the fear away. For example, I continuously have to find humorous or easier ways to neutralize information to my patients when we are talking about sensitive behaviors they need to change. Another good example of neutralizing fear is having to tell patients about the risk of cognitive impairment after surgery.

People share that they understand why I do this when we debrief after their situation changes. Laugh like there is nothing wrong in your life. Laugh like there is no tomorrow. Laugh and many will join you.

Laughter is reassuring. No matter what we go through in life things have a way of getting better. Knowing that tomorrow will come and has it's own joys and opportunities is a reason to laugh. Laughter helps reassure your tomorrow, and helps you focus on the good coming your way. For that moment, you are reassured better.

Laughter relaxes you. Medical doctors say humor allows the heart to relax. The act of laughing causes you to take in more oxygen, which is good for your heart, lungs and muscles. Laughing increases your brain's release of endorphins, making you feel good and giving you a sense of euphoria. A good laugh relaxes you, it eases tension and relieves stress.

10. Exercising Will Help Keep Your Attitude Positive

One of the best ways to move to a more positive and motivated frame of mind is to exercise. Trust me I hated hearing just the word, "exercise" until I was diagnosed with diabetes and high blood pressure. Boy, I really did get off my butt and started exercising.

I Love to walk. I am blessed to be in a neighborhood with a walkway, trees and water where the walk in itself is not only relaxing but soothing. I walk in the mornings, what a great way to start my days. I feel so good, it keeps my attitude upbeat and in turn helping me manage diabetes. A regular excise routine can provide relatively quick, positive feedback in the form of weight loss, muscle development and a sense of doing something positive for yourself. It is no secret that life seems to reward us most when we approach the world with a positive attitude.

Attitude is Everything.

How does your attitude about life show up in the world? In your thinking? In your actions? In your interaction with others?

_____

_____

_____

_____

_____

_____

_____

_____

_____

"If you don't design your own life plan, chances are you'll fall into someone else's plan and guess what they have planned for you? Not much. - Jim Rohn ".

Dr. **Stem**

Unstoppable

Living A Free And Fearless Life

Know Your Purpose And What You Want In Life

If you really want to become unstoppable and prevent being a victim of fear, know what you want. When you are clear about what you want, fear loses much of its power. When fear loses it power, you become free. Once you become free, you become unstoppable!

If you want to be really sure about what you want out of life, you must identify your purpose. Your purpose is the thing that you were put on this earth to do. It's the thing that makes you the happiest, that you do incredibly well and effortlessly. It keeps you moving forward because it always gives you something to look forward to. It's the thing you can't imagine yourself not doing.

When you figure out what your purpose is, you know it, you feel it, you sense it, you live it, you breathe it, and there's no turning back. Don't allow fear to make you question your purpose. Once you really know what you want in life, don't second-guess yourself. Be sure of yourself and what it is you know you want.

Many people find it difficult to distinguish between finding purpose and making a living. It's possible to find your purpose in something you do while making a living that has nothing to do your job duties themselves. For example, you might find yourself being the mediator in just about every situation at work.

Though this might not be part of your job description, it's something that you know you're meant to do-- bridge people together, foster collaboration and demonstrate leadership.

Likewise, your purpose might be something inside of you that is completely separate from what you do for a living. In fact, there are people all around you who have a purpose outside of their "9 to 5". People discover their purpose and set out to fulfill it at different points in their lives. You're never too young or old to find your purpose and act upon it.

Acting upon it is where most people fall short because of fear. It's not until you start walking in your purpose that you go from being fearless to free.

"It's your place in the world; it's your life. Go on and do all you can with it, and make it the life you want to live".

– Mae Jemison

Self- Reflection
Know Your Purpose & What You Want In Life

To be unstoppable you definitely have to commit time and money to discover your purpose. When you have a purpose in life, you express it constantly and base your decisions, thoughts, feelings and actions around that overarching purpose.

A person who knows their purpose tends to make a greater impact through their work, which encourages a feeling of gratification.

One of my mentors, Oprah Winfrey, said:

"There's no greater gift than to honor your life's calling. It's why you were born. And how you become most truly alive."– Oprah Winfrey

Just in case you are one of those people wondering why knowing or finding your purpose is key in life, here are some of the reasons why finding your purpose is important.

1. Purpose helps you stay focused

When you know your life's purpose, it becomes easier to focus on what matters the most in your life. By keeping the focus on one particular goal, you are able to find your direction and stay away from distractions.

2. Purpose makes you feel passionate about your goal

Knowing your purpose helps you find your true passion, and the passion becomes an important driver for you to achieve something extraordinary. Whether it is a childhood dream or a newly adopted lifestyle, the passion will push you to reach your goals.

3. Purpose gives your life clarity

People who know their purpose in life are unstoppable. They are true to their purpose and shape their life accordingly. People who don't know their purpose in life are not clear about what they want, and therefore waste their time on futile things.

4. Purpose makes you feel gratified

When you have a purpose in life, you express it constantly and base your decisions, thoughts, feelings and actions around that overarching purpose. A person who knows their purpose tends to make a greater impact through their work, which encourages a feeling of gratification.

5. Purpose enables you to live a value-based life

With purpose come values, which are an integral aspect of our lives. Values are the rules that guide our decisions in life and help define our goals. They are what tells us when we're on the right path or wrong path, and help us find and connect with others who share our way of viewing the world.

6. Purpose makes you live with integrity

Knowing your purpose in life helps you live life with integrity. People who know their purpose in life know who they are, and why they are. And when you know yourself, and have purpose, it becomes easier to live a life that's true to your core values.

Purpose encourages trust

People who know their purpose say things seem to go a lot easier. They seem to get what they want easier with little to no effort sometimes. It means they love what they are pursuing so much that it becomes easy to them.

They trust all will go well because they are living on purpose. They are doing what they love, they are with people they love, and they are living the life they love. With all this comes a deepening of trust and faith in other people. Hence they consider themselves an integral part of the universe.

Purpose infuses an element of grace in your life

People living their life with a purpose often say they are living their life with grace. Just hearing the word, "grace", you know they are at peace. The purpose of life is not to be happy.

It is to be useful, to be honorable, to be compassionate, to have it make some difference that you have lived and lived well."

"The purpose of life is to live it, to taste experience to the utmost, to reach out eagerly and without fear for newer and richer experience." When you commit to living your life with a purpose, amazing things can happen.

Purpose helps you find a flow in life

People who find their purpose tend to live in the flow of the universal stream of consciousness. They allow things to happen and change in their life rather than fighting against it. They tend to challenge themselves and battle against their fears. Fears become paper thin.

You realize there is nothing to fear. You realize whatever you want to do or achieve is doable because others have done it. You realize that fear costs you life, time, joy, money and opportunities.

Purpose makes life even more fun

When people know their purpose in life, they enjoy every minute of it. I am. I know. I am able to take pleasure in living a purpose-driven life, enjoying every moment of empowering and encouraging others everyday of my life.

I am better at tackling every situation in a creative way because I am on purpose and it is easier to deal with situations. Even the dullest thing becomes beautiful and creative because I am motivated by my purpose.

Δ Do you know what your purpose is in life? What is the thing that makes you the happiest, that you do incredibly well and can't imagine yourself not doing?

_____
_____
_____
_____
_____
_____
_____

Δ **Why is your purpose important to you? What about it brings you meaning?**

_____

_____

_____

_____

_____

_____

_____

SELF-WORTH

One of the ways to defeat fear is knowing your self worth Once you identify your purpose and what you want out of life, you have to believe that you're worth it! It's so easy for us to tell ourselves, "You're not good enough" or "You don't have what it takes", but thoughts like these are merely symptoms of fear. It's what we tell ourselves because we're too afraid to try and fail.

One of the most freeing things you can do is believe in yourself. You have to know that you are worth believing and investing in. It doesn't matter how many mistakes you may have made in the past or how unworthy you might feel, you're worth fulfilling your purpose for one reason and one reason only--no one else can fulfill your purpose but you.

Your purpose is not contingent upon your background, what degrees you have, where you were raised, your age or how much money you have. Your purpose is contingent upon you. It does not have prerequisites; it only requires you to show up.

That is why it's so important to know you who are, because when you know who you are, you know your worth. And when you know your worth, you value yourself enough to put in the necessary work.

Sadly, there are many people who have great vision and work very hard to achieve it, but to no avail because they're working toward something without ever believing that they are worth what they're trying to accomplish. If you don't believe in you, no one else will. Most importantly, if you don't believe in you, you'll never have the capacity to give what you're working toward your all.

Your self-doubt will always be there to hold you back—subtly reminding you that you're not worth what you're trying to do, until one day you realize you've been working toward something but not at your greatest potential, simply because you didn't know your own self worth.

Without self-worth, it's hard to show up at all because not believing in yourself means you've already been defeated. Whatever your purpose is in life, whatever it is you want to pursue, you're worth it!

"You were given this life because you're strong enough to live it".

Self- Reflection

Self-Worth

The dictionary defines self-worth as "the sense of one's own value or worth as a person." However, there are many ways for a person to value themselves and assess their worth as a human being, some of which are more psychologically beneficial than others.

Self-worth is how we feel about ourselves, how we think about ourselves, and how we act toward ourselves.

Boosting Your Self-Worth
We talk a lot about self-esteem. Here we are talking about self -worth, your worthiness. Boost your self-worth takes several steps. The first step in boosting self-worth is to stop comparing yourself to others and evaluating your every move; in other words, you need to challenge your critical inner voice.

The critical inner voice is like a nasty coach in our heads that constantly nags us with destructive thoughts towards ourselves or others. This is what brings up negative situations and feelings when you least expect to. I know I keep bringing this up. It is that important, trust me. A lot of what prevents most people from living an unstoppable life is how they think and feel.

It is the inner dialogue they have which in turn affects their self-worth and abilities. The reason why it is so important to tame this inner voice is because inner voices undermine our sense of self-worth and even lead to self-destruction. It can make people stay in a state of content even when they are not happy where they are.

Δ Has there ever been a time when you didn't feel worthy of something you wanted to achieve in life? Why? How did it impact your ability to succeed?

_____

_____

_____

_____

_____

_____

Δ **What things can you do remind yourself of your self-worth?**

_____

_____

_____

_____

_____

_____

_____

"It's not what you say out of your mouth that determines your life, it's what you whisper to yourself that has the most power. i".

– Robert T. Kiyosaki

"Always ask yourself if what you're doing today is getting you closer to where you want to be tomorrow." - Paulo Coelho

Dr. **Stem**

Unstoppable

Living A Free And Fearless Life

Self Efficacy And Self Confidence

Beyond believing that you're worth what you want out of life, you must believe that you can do it. You must believe that you are capable of achieving whatever it is that you want to accomplish. Even if you feel like you're worth it, if you don't have the confidence that you can do it, you're already defeated.

You must believe that you have the "know- how", the skills, the expertise, the talent or whatever it takes to get there. Even if you don't currently possess the skills and expertise that some of the colleagues or associates around you who are excelling have, you must have the confidence that you are capable of obtaining the necessary skills and expertise.

In some cases, your talent might be so great that what the people around you needed to be a success might not be required of you because your capability speaks for itself. It's important to demonstrate to yourself and others around you that you have what it takes. Walk with your head high, don't shy away from sharing what you know because you feel inferior. Take advantage of opportunities to share your knowledge and demonstrate your talent. Demonstrate that you are self-sufficient and confident in your abilities.

There are people who actually have lots of skills but lack the confidence they need to be effective.
These are people who have the required knowledge but are so incapable of being self- efficient, they require lots of "hand-holding".

Be confident in yourself and your ability to be independent. Don't fall for the trap of believing that the only way you can make it is if someone else does it for you. You are fully capable! This doesn't mean you won't need a little help or mentoring along the way. We all need advice and guidance at some point or another. In fact, it's critical to our success.

However, you should never limit your ability to succeed to another person's belief in your abilities. Most importantly, you can't limit your success by not believing in your own abilities. You can do it, and you must be determined that you will!

"If you don't go after what you want, you'll never have it. If you don't ask, the answer is always no. If you don't step forward, you're always in the same place".

–Nora Roberts

SELF- REFLECTION
SELF EFFICACY AND SELF CONFIDENCE

A lot of people get confused with the difference between self-efficacy and self-confidence. **Self-efficacy** refers to beliefs about one's ability to perform specific tasks (e.g., driving, public speaking, studying, etc.) **Self-confidence** refers to belief in one's personal worth and likelihood of succeeding. Self-confidence is a combination of self-esteem and general self-efficacy.

Self-efficacy

Self-efficacy is therefore your belief in your own abilities to deal with various situations. It can play a role in not only how you feel about yourself, but whether or not you successfully achieve your goals in life. Almost all people can identify goals they want to accomplish, things they would like to change, and things they would like to achieve.

However, most people also realize that putting these plans into action is not quite so simple. Psychologist Bandura and others have in their studies found that an individual's self-efficacy plays a major role in how goals, tasks, and challenges are approached.

People with a strong sense of self-efficacy:
- View challenging problems as tasks to be mastered
- Develop deeper interest in the activities in which they participate
- Form a stronger sense of commitment to their interests and activities
- Recover quickly from setbacks and disappointments

People with a weak sense of self-efficacy:
- Avoid challenging tasks
- Believe that difficult tasks and situations are beyond their capabilities
- Focus on personal failings and negative outcomes
- Quickly lose confidence in personal abilities

Let's see if you have a strong self-efficacy by answering the following questions:
- Do you feel like you can handle problems if you are willing to work hard?
- Are you confident in your ability to achieve your goals?
- Do you feel like you can manage unexpected events that come up?

- Are you able to bounce back fairly quickly after stressful events?
- Do you feel like you can come up with solutions when you are facing a problem?
- Do you keep trying even when things seem difficult?
- Are you good at staying calm even in the face of chaos?
- Do you perform well even under pressure?
- Do you tend to focus on your progress rather than getting overwhelmed by all you still have to do?
- Do you believe that hard work will eventually pay off?

If you can answer yes to many or most of these questions, then chances are good that you have a fairly strong sense of self-efficacy

Boosting Your Self-Efficacy

Let's have you become unstoppable. Boosting your self-efficacy makes you believe in yourself more, gives you the courage to try many things and to stay the course when the going gets tough.

1. Celebrate Your Success
When you succeed at something, you are able to build a powerful belief in your ability. So, work on setting goals that are achievable, but not necessarily easy. Take time to celebrate your successes.

2. Observe and Learn From Others

Seeing others putting in effort and succeeding at what they do can increase your belief in your own ability to succeed. This is a big self-efficacy booster because, once you observe others do it, you know it is definitely possible for you do it too.

3. Seek Positive People and Positive Affirmations

Hearing positive feedback from others can also help improve your sense of self-efficacy. By that same token, try to avoid asking for feedback from people who you know are more likely to have a negative or critical view of your performance. Positive social feedback can be helpful for strengthening your already existing sense of efficacy. Say positive affirmations, they boost both your self-efficacy and self-confidence.

Δ Have you ever stalled on doing something you wanted to do because you convinced yourself that you didn't have what it takes? How did this impact you?

_____

_____

_____

_____

_____

Self-Confidence

Self-confidence is a feeling of trust in your abilities, qualities, and judgment. I love this quote because it says it all. "Once we believe in ourselves, we can risk curiosity, wonder, spontaneous delight, or any experience that reveals the human spirit." – E.E. Cummings

Self-confidence brings about more happiness. Typically, when you are confident in your abilities you are happier due to your successes and interactions with others. Also, when you are feeling better about your capabilities, You are more energized and motivated to take action and achieve your goals.

Self-confidence is similar to self-efficacy in that it tends to focus on future performance; however, it seems to be based on prior performance. So in a sense, it also focuses on the past. so you can always look back and see what you can be happy about or proud of to boost your confidence.

Self-confidence is good for you because of following reasons among the many reasons I can list.

    A greater sense of self-worth.
    Greater enjoyment in life and in activities
    Freedom from self-doubt

Freedom from fear and anxiety, freedom from social anxiety, and less stress

More energy and motivation to act

Have a more enjoyable time talking to other people at social gatherings. When you are relaxed and confident others will feel at ease around you.

Boosting Your Self-Confidence

1) Do More Things You're Good at or Improve at Things You're Not
2) Do Good Things for Others
3) Be Authentic
4) Do Things You Feel Good About
5) Be in the Right Environment, Work, Home, Community.
6) Dress To Be Addressed
7) Dress Like You Are Already Doing That Dream Job
8) Be Gentle with Yourself
9) Be Gentle with Your Self Talk and Thoughts
10) Celebrate Small Wins
11) Ignore the Haters
12) Never Let Anyone Rain on Your Parade
13) Say "Bye Felicia" Often
14) Think Big

15) Believe Big
16) Be Your Number One Cheerleader
17) Know You Are Unique and Special
18) You Deserve Better Only if You Believe it and Ask
19) You are Unstoppable

People will at times express their own lack of self-confidence by trying to tear down yours. Instead of letting them get in your head, learn how to deal with them. Only those who are hurting, try to hurt other people. It is also a sign that you are doing something notable. People don't bother hating on those that have no impact. So keep on keeping on. Do You. Confidence is within you.

Δ What would you tell yourself about your self-confidence then, knowing what you know now? How can you continue to build your self-confidence?

_____

_____

_____

_____

_____

_____

_____

When you do the common things in life in an uncommon way, you will command the attention of the world."
George Washington Carver".

Dr. **Stem**

Unstoppable
Living A Free And Fearless Life

Vision And Goals

Once you've identified your purpose and have the confidence that you can do it, you're more than half way there. However, it's important to have a vision and goals for what you want to achieve if you truly want to be unstoppable.

This is true for a few reasons.

First, having a vision helps to eliminate distractions because you know exactly what you're striving toward and why. When you know what you want, you're less likely to be sidetracked.

Second, goals allow you to identify the outcomes you want to achieve so that you can realize your overall vision.

Third, having a vision and goals provides you with a road map for how to achieve your vision so that you don't waste a lot of time trying to find direction.

So, what exactly is a vision and how does it differ from your goals? Visions are unlimited in nature and cannot be measured. They are simply what you imagine for yourself and your life. Your vision can be as big and audacious as you'd like. In fact, they should be!

When you establish a vision for what you want your life to be, don't put any limits on it. It might feel ridiculous at first because we're prone to think about why our ultimate vision wouldn't work-- we can't afford it, we don't have time, we don't have the experience--the list goes on and on. However, your vision should be your purpose's best friend. You wouldn't put a limit on your purpose, so why would you limit your vision?

Think big, think fearless, let your imagination free. Goals, unlike vision, are actionable and measurable. Once you understand what your vision is, you can establish realistic goals for how you might achieve your ultimate vision. Though your goals for realizing your vision should be realistic, be careful not to limit yourself in establishing your goals based on what you think you can and can't do. Be audacious, even in setting your goals, and get creative in thinking of ways to achieve them.

Don't let fear stop you from doing this. The minute you allow fear to interfere with the goals you set for yourself, you've already set yourself back before even getting started. You might be thinking, "what do I do if I can't seem to figure out a way to make my goal realistic?" Don't allow yourself to think about what you can't do and focus on what you can do.

Explore every option, every possibility, and think of possibilities for achieving something that might not even have been attempted before. Remember, you are in control of your vision, what it looks like and how it's carried out.

Keep in mind that your goals serve as a roadmap for where you ultimately want to be. Just like any map, you can change direction and reroute whenever you feel necessary.

Your map doesn't have to be perfect. There's no such thing as a map with consistently straight lines. Any reliable roadmap has a plethora of colors, signs, twists and turns. Even if your goals seem to be far-fetched and all over the place, write them down so that you can begin to organize your thoughts and pin- point the best route to reach your destination.

You have the freedom to determine the who, what, where and when. You should be fearless, even in establishing your vision and goals.

Self- Reflection
Vision And Goals

A goal is a specific target to achieve something. ... A goal is achievable. A vision on the other hand is "out there" it seems totally unachievable, but we aspire to it anyway. It is important to set and achieve goals that promote and are in line with your vision.

This is why, if you don't have a vision, goals alone can be defeating (i.e., without a vision, each goal is just something you've completed without a larger "why" in mind).

∆ What is the vision you have for your life? What would you like to ultimately accomplish? What would you consider to be your life goal?

_____

_____

_____

_____

_____

Δ **What are some goals you need to achieve in order to realize your vision? What steps do you need to take to complete your roadmap?**

_____

_____

_____

_____

_____

_____

_____

o be a star, you must shine your own light, follow your own path, and don't worry about darkness, for that is when the stars shine brightest.

– Napoleon Hill.

"If one advances confidently in the direction of his dreams, and endeavors to live the life which he has imagined, he will meet with a success unexpected in common hours." Henry David Thoreau

Dr. **Stem**

Unstoppable
Living A Free And Fearless Life

Emotional Competence

In the same manner that you maintain confidence in your abilities, you must maintain emotional competence if you want to be unstoppable in life. Emotional competence is huge! Yet, many people underestimate its power to help them achieve success.

Emotional competence is about how you recognize, understand, express and regulate your own emotions, as well as that of others when interacting with them. You must be able to understand and regulate your emotion if you want to be free and fearless.

You can have an amazing vision, the perfect road map in terms of goals, and all of the skills and talent in the world, but if you're unable to regulate your emotions, it will all crumble. This is because our emotions drive our actions. In other words, if your emotions are unstable, it will impact the stability of everything we do.

For example, if you have an emotion of self- pity, you'll likely make excuses for why you can't do certain things or why it would never work. Likewise, if you have emotions of bitterness about something that didn't go your way in the past, you will likely be reluctant to try certain things again.

It is incredibly important that you identify your emotions, explore why you feel the way you feel, and express them in a way that is productive. This is especially important when working with others to achieve your goals. No one wants to work with a person who cannot effectively express themselves.

For example, it's difficult to accomplish anything with a person who is closed, never open to suggestions, bitter, not trusting, uncommunicative or combative. This is counterproductive to building effective relationships and achieving your goals.

Many of our emotions are a result of what we subject ourselves to. This is why it's important to nurture yourself spiritually and emotionally. If you subject yourself to constant drama and negativity, your emotional state will be damaged, and your emotional capacity will remain limited.

When you recognize your emotions and seek to understand them, you prevent your emotions from overshadowing what it is that you're trying to accomplish.

Self- Reflection
Emotional Competence

This is your ability to express or release your inner feelings (emotions). It implies an ease around others and determines your ability to effectively and successfully lead and express yourself.

Δ How good are you at recognizing your emotions? Do you brush them aside and pretend they don't exist, or do you address them head on?

_____
_____
_____
_____
_____
_____
_____
_____

Δ How good are you at regulating your emotions? Can you keep your emotions in tact when issues arise, or do you allow them to take over? How has your ability to regulate your emotions impacted you?

_____

_____

_____

_____

_____

_____

_____

Emotional Strongholds: Overcoming Doubt And More

The biggest contributors to emotional incompetence are emotional strongholds. Emotional strongholds are a collection of thoughts that negatively impact our emotions and precede our actions. These strongholds can be distracting and even damaging if not addressed.

Many times, strongholds develop because we allow certain emotions to fester without acknowledging and addressing them, resulting in the emotion becoming habitual, and sometimes, a matter of dependency. This stems from the fear of letting go of a certain emotion because it is so familiar. However, you'll never be unstoppable as long as your strongholds exist. Let's explore some common emotional strongholds.

Self-doubt is a stronghold that trains us to believe that we're not capable of doing something or that were not good enough. This is very closely tied to our self-worth. As discussed earlier, if we don't believe we're worthy of something, we allow ourselves to doubt our own abilities.

Self-doubt can also creep in if you've failed at something in the past. You might find yourself saying, "I didn't succeed the first time. Why would I succeed now?" This is a grave distraction because, many times, there are lessons to be learned from previous failures that actually help us to succeed.

Self-doubt also comes from a fear of rejection. The idea that something won't work or that someone won't support your dream can be daunting. However, you can't allow what may or may not happen keep you from trying. Like self-doubt, some people fear rejection because they've been rejected before. But this shouldn't stop you from moving forward.

You wouldn't stop driving your car because your key didn't work one time. You wouldn't stop drinking water because you spilled it on your shirt once. You wouldn't stop buying shoes because you once purchased a pair with a bad sole or broken heel. No, you would simply readjust. You would turn the key to your car in another direction or have it repaired.

You'd be careful not to drink your water too fast, and you'd purchase quality shoes with more durability.

Self-doubt also gives us an excuse not to do something so that we don't have to leave our comfort zone. It also causes us to adopt a victim mentality or fall victim to defeatism.

This is when you convince yourself that you can't succeed because everything or everyone is against you, when, in fact, it's just an excuse not to try, or a protective mechanism to keep us from being hurt when we fail.

It's so much easier to make everything else the blame, rather than take responsibility for our own actions. However, you can't be fearless if you're not willing to be vulnerable. This includes being vulnerable to mistakes, rejection, or even failure. Remember, failure is subjective. There's often something to be learned when things don't go as planned to help us perfect our efforts moving forward.

You must learn to step out of your comfort zone. The road to becoming fearless is not always comfortable! If you are going to make it through this journey successfully, you are going to have to push your own limits. You will never grow if you continue to do only what you're familiar with. In fact, many find that the more pressure and discomfort they experience during their journey, the greater the reward.

Hopelessness is another form of defeatism that serves as a major stronghold. When you convince yourself that there's no hope for something to succeed or that you are completely helpless, you've coddled yourself so that you don't have to try or subject yourself to the unknown. Hopelessness is a tactic of fear. Fear is the enemy of hope because you need hope to dream, to have vision, to set goals and believe that you can achieve them.

You need hope to take action with the anticipation that you will succeed.

Sometimes, life presents us with so many disappointments that it's hard not to feel hopeless. However, it's important not to get stuck here. Determine that you will achieve your goals, no matter what comes your way. Hold onto your self-confidence and maintain a will to succeed as though your life depends on it.

Worry is another major emotional stronghold that can stifle you from accomplishing anything. Worry is often an unnecessary and unrealistic concern that we create to protect ourselves from things that might go wrong. It is a form of anxiety that is also born out of fear. If you worry about something enough, you'll never take action. Rather than becomingfearless, you become fearful of just about everything.
Even when you have reasonable cause for concern, it's important that you recognize and address it so that you can move forward, rather than use it as an excuse not to take action.

Sometimes our strongholds can be our own egos, resulting in stubbornness and pride. Wanting to do everything your way without being open to advice or change is a recipe for disaster. The world around us is constantly evolving, which means there are always new and more effective ways to accomplish things. The journey to becoming fearless requires a willingness to learn and grow. Stubbornness restrains you from doing this.

Pride is similar to stubbornness in that it doesn't allow you to take direction from anyone or be open to ideas to anything other than your own due to the belief that you are the "end all, be all". This results in you becoming self-absorbed and ignorant to the people and things around you. This is also the fastest way to be left behind.

There's nothing wrong with being proud of your talents and accomplishments, but unlike self- confidence, too much pride leads you to believe that you have no need for improvement or that your knowledge is somehow superior to that of others. Like the previous strongholds, this is done out of fear—fear that someone else could be better or outshine you, fear that you will no longer be seen as the expert.

However, letting go of stubbornness and pride demonstrates just the opposite; it demonstrates that you have the wisdom to learn and grow.

Another crippling stronghold is the fear of other people's opinions. So many people never achieve their full potential because they're too afraid of what other people might say or think. The story usually goes, "What if they think I'm crazy?

What if they think I don't have what it takes? What if they laugh about my ideas?

What if they talk about me behind my back? What if they don't support me?" No one's opinion about your future is more important than yours.

Never allow anyone's perception or opinion about your vision deter you from going after your dream! The minute you do this, you put your destiny in the hands of other people. You are in control of your destiny, no one else. At times, we are much more concerned about what other people might think than we need to be because, where we think we might find opposition, we might actually find support. Even if you encounter negativity, it shouldn't serve as a roadblock to your success.

Remember, you're in the driver seat. Everyone else should be in the passenger or back seat. Some people don't need to be in the car at all. Learn to let go of other people's opinions and focus on your purpose. Other people's opinion of you are not greater than your purpose.

How do you conquer emotional strongholds? Give yourself permission to live in your purpose! When you give yourself permission to do this, your strongholds begin to lose their power. Making a commitment to choose your purpose and vision over your stronghold takes practice, but it can be done. The key is to make your strongholds less habitual.

Don't make it a habit to rely on your emotion. Make it a habit to relay on your purpose, instead. Once you do this, your strongholds cease to be strongholds at all. The more you choose your purpose, the less you choose the emotion that once contributed to your stronghold.

"Success is walking from failure to failure with no loss of enthusiasm."

– Winston Churchill

SELF-REFLECTION
EMOTIONAL STRONGHOLDS: OVERCOMING DOUBT AND MORE

Emotional strongholds come in all shapes and sizes-- doubt, rejection, poor self-esteem, pride, stubbornness, a victim mentality, or defeatism.

Doubt robs us of joy, confidence and hope, sending us spiraling from a self-assured state of mind to one of worry, self-consciousness and uncertainty.

To overcome Self-doubt and let go of emotional holds, here are a few tips:

1. Believe in yourself
2. Be willing to change course.
3. Fall and get back up
4. Decide and Do
5. Dig deep into your values, faith and beliefs
6. Teach others overcome self-doubt-you will gain more from teaching
7. Remove yourself from toxic situations, physically, mentally and spiritually

8. Remember too much of anything is not good for you, pace yourself.
9. Take time for self-care and mental breaks.
10. Be willing to be honest with yourself and open up to others about how you feel.
11. Know the signs of doubt and be willing to fight back.
12. Always stick to your values and morals.
13. Rely on your past successes, you can do it again.
14. You have to believe in what's possible.
15. Don't let your fear fail you.
16. Stay away from being a critic of others when they fail.
17. Remember doubt strikes everyone, it is how you handle it that matters.
18. Aim to prove Doubt Wrong and Go For it.
19. Feel the doubt and do it anyway.

Δ **What are some emotional strongholds you've struggled with in the past?**

_____

_____

_____

_____

_____

How have they hindered you from living your best life?

_____
_____
_____
_____
_____
_____
_____

Are there any that you still struggle with today?

_____
_____
_____
_____
_____
_____
_____

Identify your most powerful emotional stronghold and describe how you plan to take away its power over your life?

_____

_____

_____

_____

_____

_____

_____

"Strength does not come from physical capacity. It comes from an indomitable will."

- Mahatma Gandhi

"I learned that courage was not the absence of fear, but the triumph over it. The brave man is not he who does not feel afraid, but he who conquers that fear. Nelson Mandela"

Dr. **Stem**

Unstoppable

Living A Free And Fearless Life

Developing A Fearless Mindset: What It Means To Be Bold And Fearless

If you want to be fearless, you must develop a fearless mindset. You may have heard that the mind is a terrible thing to waste. Worst than this, it is a terrible thing to restrain with fear.

Your mind is designed to think and create. It cannot create if it is restricted by fear. It takes a conscious effort to develop a fearless mindset; it does not come easy. However, the more you commit to establishing this mindset and putting it into practice, the more natural it will become.

Start by eliminating distractions. What are the things in your life that make your vision an afterthought? What are the things that sidetrack you even after you decide to focus on your vision? What is it that's causing you doubt? What are you doing that's occupying your time and energy unnecessarily?

Are you doing things to tie up your money unnecessarily that you could be using to invest in your dream?

Once you identify these things, make a conscious decision not to make them priority over your vision. Don't let worry or doubt creep in. Trust that your purpose will make a way for you. Spend time focusing on your vision where you might otherwise spend it doing other activities, such as watching television, scrolling through your phone, or on surfing the internet. Make your vision the priority and everything else a part of the background.

Be more responsible with your finances. Don't spend your money on any and everything. The same is true when it comes to people—don't spend all of your money trying to help any and everybody. This might sound harsh, but it's a necessary rule to follow. You will need to shift your thinking to utilizing your finances to help you achieve your success so that, in the long-run, you can help some of the people you want to help and purchase the things you want.

Remain positive. Don't fill your head with negative thoughts or what could go wrong. Instead, think of all the wonderful things that will come with realizing your vision. Read motivational books, listen to motivational music, and give yourself positive affirmations. Remind yourself that you are worth it, you can do it, and commit to not backing down. Give yourself a daily dose of motivation, just as you would take a daily vitamin or eat a healthy meal. It is important to nourish yourself, heart, mind and soul.

The people you surround yourself with are just as important as the thoughts you subject yourself to. Don't surround yourself with negative people. These are people who do nothing but criticize, complain, diminish your hope or create doubt. Often times, these are also people who aren't interested in bettering themselves; they focus more on what everyone else is doing. This is the absolute worst company you can keep when trying to achieve a major life goal.

It's important that you surround yourself with people who will motivate and inspire you, provide constructive feedback, support you mentally and emotionally, and encourage you to keep moving forward—even at times when you feel like giving up. It's also critically important that you not compare yourself with other people's success.

Never compare yourself to anyone else. Be yourself and never try to conform to anyone else's expectations. Everyone has a unique purpose with its own unique timing. This is why comparing your success to that of others is misleading. It is also dangerous in that it distracts you from moving in the direction you need to be moving in. If you notice someone achieving success in an area that interests you, it's ok to seek them for advice. In fact, you should surround with successful people because it might help you avoid some common pitfalls.

However, be careful not to mimic their journey or compare their timing and results to your own. Your journey is not meant to be the same as anyone else's.

Be bold by countering fear with courage. Prove to yourself that you have the courage to overcome, to push forward and conquer what you've set out to do during the times when you feel the most fearful. This is how you approach fear head on and put it on it's back. The trick is to not approach fear with being fearful, it's just the opposite—being courageous.

This will require you to leave your comfort zone, but don't shy away from it. A good example of this is when astronauts take off into space. The initial launch is filled with pressure and discomfort, but once they arrive into space, they float—completely free from the pressure that initially caused their discomfort. Furthermore, where they were once looking at their immediate surroundings, they now have a much broader view of the world.

The morale of the story here is, if you want to broaden your horizons and achieve what you've envisioned for your life, you must launch, no matter how afraid or uncomfortable you might be.

A fearless mindset is one that is constantly open to learning and exploring new ideas. The minute you decide there's nothing more you need to learn is the minute your journey to becoming your best self will come to an end. A fearless mindset requires you not to be afraid to learn something new or adopt new ways of doing things. It can be scary to try something different because it makes us uncomfortable.

But, remember, being fearless is all about leaving your comfort zone. The more you learn, the more you'll grow, and the more effective you'll be in achieving what you've set out to do. You must be bold and take risks. This doesn't mean you have to be a "bully" or careless.

Being bold is often mistaken as being someone who is overly direct or ruthless. Likewise, taking risks can be mistaken as being careless or irresponsible. However, this couldn't be farther from the truth. It's possible to be bold in your choices and maintain humility. Likewise, it's possible to take calculated risks responsibly. It's ok to approach decisions conservatively and make practical choices. However, don't allow practical to be your comfort zone.

Being fearless will require you to push the envelope, beyond what you think you can do or what seems possible. Even if you've already taken a few risks here and there, be careful not to become complacent. You must always push yourself further. The more you put yourself out there, the more fearless you'll become.

Remember, a fearless mindset is one that does not cease to grow. A fearless mindset is also one that is consistent. It's the mindset of not giving up. No matter how challenging your journey might become in your quest to fulfill your vision, you must keep going. This might seem cliché, but it's necessary. Many people fall short of their life goals, not because they were incapable, but because they simply give up.

Imagine if the Wright brothers had given up on trying to invent an airplane. We wouldn't be able to travel the world with such ease. Imagine if Steve Jobs had given up on trying to revolutionize computer technology. Many of us wouldn't have iphones or Apple products as we know them today. Imagine if Barack Obama had given up on becoming president. We wouldn't have seen the first African-American president in our lifetime.

If you think any of these pillars in history didn't face challenges or even moments where they were tempted to throw in the towel, think again! They made a conscious decision to keep pushing forward, in spite of their challenges.

Self- Reflection
Developing A Fearless Mindset: What It Means To Be Bold & Fearless

We all have fear – it's an emotion that's as normal as breathing. The problem is that most people hold onto their fears, and are therefore unable to move forward in their lives with necessary change.

I have learned a lot about fear in my counseling and coaching business. I've learned that the only difference between people who achieve greatness and those who do not is those who achieve greatness discarded their fear. They chose to not focus on their fears or to even acknowledge it and give it more attention than it deserves.

Below are some of the tips I have used to get to this "Unstoppable Free and Fearless State" in my Life.

1. Admit to your fear(s). Be aware of fear in your life. Before you can begin overcoming fear, you have to admit that you have fear. Know the triggers, those indications that show up before or when you are afraid. Write down some aspects of your life where you have fear; writing them on paper is important, because trying to simply think them through never works.

2. Look for fearless people. Fill your brain with images of what you want your "future self" to look like. Connect with as many role models as you can, whether in person, through a book, or online. Use these examples as an energy source to combat your fear.

3. Be an objective observer of your own life. Be objective. Take an interest in investigating your fears. Ask yourself about what thoughts generate your fear, where you feel the fear, and how you react to it. That is being an objective observer of your own life.

4. Be willing to risk the emotional pain of making mistakes Be willing to look stupid. Once you are willing to risk the emotional pain of making mistakes, you will shed more fear than you ever imagined. Know that making mistakes will help you obtain information you use to develop corrective behaviors, and that everyone who has ever done something great has failed more than once.

5. Be grateful for the opportunities. Adopt a mindset of gratitude. Whenever you feel fear, try to feel grateful instead. Whenever I get fearful I now ask myself "What is the worst thing that could happen?" A true evaluation of all possibilities tells me nothing serious could happen so I step over my fears and do just it.

6. Seek out great coaches/teachers. It's never too late to have a teacher or coach, because we are never done learning. I have a coach I love very much because she is a no-nonsense coach and teacher. Seek out someone who scares you a little—not a polite person who always makes you feel warm and fuzzy. Seek out someone who watches you closely, is brutally honest, and gives clear directions on how you can get better at whatever scares you.

My best friend Dr John Loblack is my "scary coach". He does not hold back. I appreciate him more today than ever before. We used to be at odds a lot because he tells me like it is. That kind of teaching makes you grow. I didn't know it before, but now I appreciate it, as I have seen the growth in me.

7. Confide and share with someone. How often do we hold the negative in because we are afraid of how others might react? Sharing helps, because you will realize that many people feel the same way as you do and have stories to share, as well. Do you have a fear of success, or a fear of failure? Sharing with someone can help you examine what you truly want from life, and where your fears come from.

8. Embrace Challenges and Struggle. Most of us instinctively avoid struggle, because it feels like failure, and that scares us, but the phrase "no pain, no gain" holds true. To develop our skills, it is a necessity that we face challenges and struggle, so we must embrace both the challenges and struggle. Once we overcome those two, fear slowly disintegrates.

9. Enjoy reading a book. Reading a good book never goes out of fashion. Reading opens new doors on how you can get rid of doubt and fear. I constantly fill my world with motivational and inspirational books and audio books, related to, the topic I'm dealing with.

10. Visualize Your desired Outcomes instead of your doubt and fears. Use visualization. Imagine yourself in a scary situation without fear. Watch people do things fearlessly that would normally freak you out. Visualize yourself as that person. Create a very clear picture of fearlessness in your mind.

11. Be Real. Put things in perspective. Putting your negative thoughts in perspective is a huge way to overcome fear. In the grand scheme of life, why are you afraid? While you are freaking out about something, life is moving on without you.

Sometimes it's helpful to remember this.

12. Let go of control. Release control. I know we all want to be in control, but when we relinquish it we tend to free ourselves up. Allow yourself to make mistakes—after all, that's where learning and growth really happens. We learn from our failures, but to fail we need to release control.

13. Life Goes On. Think about the worst-case scenario. What's the worst that could happen? I have crumbled on stage in front of hundreds of people. I still did well and am alive. I lived. Life goes on.

14. Take a Good Look within. What is the root of your fear? Meditate on it. Look inside and ask yourself. How far back does your fear go? Did you have an early failure that has stuck with you? Explore it. That's what life is all about.

Overcoming fear requires an attitude that knows that we can grow and change if we choose. Nothing is "locked in" forever; we can change. It takes time and practice. Hopefully the tips above will help you begin your journey to ditch fear.

When you are truly confident, you are free to act fearlessly. When you are no longer full of stress, doubts and worries, you are free, and hence, you are fearless. And when you are fearless, you feel truly amazing.

Δ **What steps have you not yet taken to develop a fearless mindset but intent to after having completed this book? How?**

_____

_____

_____

_____

_____

_____

_____

_____

I was taught that the way of progress was neither swift nor easy.

-Marie Curie

Dealing with Failure and Starting Over

Perhaps you really want to be fearless, or were once fearless, even, but you've encountered too many disappointments or failures. Don't let this stop you! Part of developing a fearless mindset requires a shift in your thinking about failure.

Let's consider the definition of failure. It's defined as a lack of success or the omission of required or expected results. You may have been the case for you, multiple times.

However, it's important to keep in mind that when we talk about failure, we are referring to a specific incident or circumstance during a specific time and place. The problem is we have the tendency to deem failure as something infinite or inevitable. Don't fall for this trap. Failure is something that happened then, not something that will always be.

So, what does this mean? This means, the meal that was overcooked last night might turn out perfectly tomorrow. The test that was failed last week might be passed with flying colors next week. The bankruptcy that was filed last year might result in surplus this year.

How? Because the temperature on the stove was readjusted for the meal, there was a lot more studying and a better understanding for what was expected in the test, and a lot more accountability associated with managing finances.

These improvements don't happen with some magic potion; they happen thanks to mistakes—messing up, getting it wrong, failing. Sometimes, it takes getting it wrong to get it right. Learn not to be so hard on yourself and ask yourself, "What can I learn from this? How could I have done this differently? How can I do this better the next time?" This is how you become unstoppable.

Some of the most fearless and most successful people are those with wisdom. Wisdom defined is the quality of having experience, knowledge, and good judgment; the quality of being wise.

It's the soundness of an action or decision with regard to the application of our experiences, knowledge, and good judgment. It's not possible to gain experience or establish good judgement if we don't open ourselves up to experiences, good and bad. How would you ever know what good judgement is if you've never made any bad decisions.

Now, don't get carried away in thinking that it's ok to make a bunch of foolish mistakes for the sake of becoming wise. You should always use good judgement when making any decision.

However, don't use your past failures as an excuse not to move forward in your journey.

Take advantage of your past mistakes and failures by using them to inform your future decisions. Think of your past experiences as a bank account. We'll call it your experience account.

This is the account you'll use to deposit lessons learned, good and bad. This is also the account you'll use to make withdrawals when faced with having to make decisions. You might have experienced one or two bounced checks, but you do not close your account. Instead, you learn to prevent those bounced checks in the future and continue to grow your account.

If you really want to be free, you cannot be afraid of failure. You must shift your thinking so that you see failure as an opportunity to learn and become wiser.

Self-Reflection
Dealing With Failure And Starting Over

One of the hardest things in life is to know when to keep going and when to move on. Life requires we be strong and confident to learn from our failures which are inevitable.

Sometimes you need to display unwavering confidence and double down on your efforts. Sometimes you need to abandon the things that aren't working and try something new. The key question is: how do you know when to give up and when to stick with it?

There is no right or wrong way of moving on after failing in anything, marriage, work, school, business, anything. Moving on after a painful breakup is, I think is the next hardest time I can recall, next to moving on after losing a loved one through death. There are days that you feel like you cannot even leave the house and that your life will never be the same.

Then you may have days where you feel so strong and think you will be OK.

It is the roller coaster that sucks so bad. About the only thing you can do is keep on breathing. The only thing you can do during the pain is to be just be sad, until you are not sad anymore".

Life is big and wide and beautiful and full of good things, no matter what happens. There is so much reason for hope. Whatever you do, don't give up. Keep searching, keeping asking, keep moving forward, even if you're moving at a snail's pace. Have Hope.

Δ Think of a time when you had to deal with failure and had a hard time starting over. How did this impact you?

_____

_____

_____

_____

_____

_____

_____

_____

What would you have done differently?

_____
_____
_____
_____
_____
_____

Describe a time when failure benefitted your success. What did you learn?

_____
_____
_____
_____
_____
_____
_____
_____

Listening and Effective Communication

We've talked a lot about the importance of learning from others and emotional competence. Both of these things require you to be an effective communicator. Many people are unable to experience being free because they are terrible at communicating.

It stunts their personal growth, professional development, and ultimately serves as a major roadblock to them becoming unstoppable. In fact, terrible communicators are often the people who experience their journey come to an end the fastest.

You might be saying to yourself, "The way that I communicate is just who I am". Well, that's just it. The way that you communicate is a reflection of you. Your personality is your personality; you are who you are. However, how you express who you are matters to your success, professionally and personally. You will not get very far if no one takes you seriously or wants to talk to you at all.

Take a good look at how you communicate with those around you and ask yourself whether it's hurting or helping you. This should be done for your family, social and business circles, because you will need to rely upon
many of these people for support and even to help open doors.

The most important communication skill you can learn is listening. This is often easier said than done. Why is listening so difficult? A few reasons. It's hard to listen when you're unable to put your own position aside during a conversation, especially if you think you're right about an issue. Even if your position is correct or perhaps more effective, the other person needs to be heard so that there's more information added to the meaning pool.

Perhaps your way is the right way, but there's a different approach that needs to be taken. On the other hand, you might think that your position is the correct one, but not realize that you're way off base until you put your position aside long enough to listen to someone else's.

Another common barrier t listening is time. We're so busy that we don't have time to listen to what others have to say. There's nothing wrong with just "getting things done", but it's counterproductive to do things without a full understanding of what comes along with it. The only way to achieve this level of understanding is by taking time to listen.

Listening can also be difficult for many people because they just want to be heard. But, remember, the person you're communicating with wants to be heard and understood, just like you. For this reason, effective communication requires a sense of empathy— the ability to understand and share the feelings of another.

Did you know that the majority of daycare and preschool providers include empathy as a skill for the assessment of emotional development? This is because educators realize that empathy is an important part of communication and survival, even in the earliest of stages. If you have no interest in understanding anyone else's emotion or point of view outside of your own, your ability to thrive is greatly reduced.

This is also why emotional competence is so important. It is very difficult to empathize if you can't understand and regulate your own emotion, as pointed out earlier.

Another skill that is required of effective communicators is active listening This requires you to not only listen, but fully concentrate, understand, respond and then remember what is being said. Active listening is more than just an occasional head nod, it's a process of interpreting and responding in a way that confirms you've heard and understood what is being said. This certainly takes practice, but is very achievable.

One of the ways to practice active listening is by repeating what you think is being said as confirmation that you understood the person talking. This reassures the person talking to you that you are indeed listening and helps to gain a level of trust amidst the conversation. This also provides an opportunity for the person talking to clarify anything you may have misunderstood.

Never jump to conclusions; always ask clarifying questions instead. Jumping to conclusions can make the person talking feel closed in or not heard, which damages mutual trust and respect. Asking clarifying questions allows you to obtain enough information to make an informed decision about an issue without it being premeditated. It also signals to the person you're talking to that you're being fair in your assessment of the issue at hand.

It also helps to check in with a person about a conversation, even after it's already been had. This adds a level of accountability, especially if the conversation resulted actionable items.

Checking in also makes you more personable. It means, not only did you understand the conversation at hand, but you also care enough about it to follow up. Demonstrate that you are indeed invested in the conversations that you have with people, and not having conversations just to hear yourself talk. For example, if someone says they'd like you help with something, don't just go on and on about how you might help or say you'll figure out a way to get together and they never hear from you again. Show that you hear and understand.

Even if you don't have the time or capability, try to connect them with someone who does, or encourage them with words of support. If it's something that isn't in line with your interests, be honest and explain why so that people understand what your intentions are. This might shed light on other areas of opportunity between you or prevent you and the other person involved from wasting time. This is what effective communication is all about.

Finally, don't be afraid to speak up. Often times, we fail to communicate because we're afraid of what we think the other person might think or feel, when, in fact, not communicating at all makes things worse. When you shy away from saying what needs to be said, you leave room for interpretation about what you feel or want done, which causes confusion.

Failure to speak up can also be misinterpreted as you not being invested in the matter at hand. It's better to be honest and contribute to the meaning pool than to not speak up at all. Speaking up doesn't mean talking over other people or taking over the conversation. It simply means contributing your thoughts and ideas, even if you're not comfortable with doing so. Being free requires you to communicate openly and honestly, yet respectfully.

The ability to communicate effectively builds trust and establishes mutual respect. The ability to do this opens doors to change, increased effectiveness and greater impact.

"You can't have a better tomorrow if you're still thinking about yesterday".
–Charles F. Kettering

Dr. **Stem**

Unstoppable
Living A Free And Fearless Life

Self- Reflection
Listening And Effective Communication

Communication is a way of speaking and listening, and understanding life. It supports us in staying engaged in life - open and curious. It is an understanding of life that inspires compassion, trust, respect, courage, acceptance, connection and strength.

Effective communication is important because it can help to foster a good relationship at home, work and communities. Effective Communication is key in relationships because without good effective communication, relationships struggle and eventually break down.

Quick tips for effective communication at home and work.
1. When communicating, always check your attitude
2. Avoid bringing up old issues
3. Take your emotions out first
4. No matter what the situation keep the conversation positive and respectful at al times.

5. No hitting below the belt
6. Own Your emotions
7. Don't exaggerate the situation
8. Remember, you will need to be in good terms again so make it civil
9. Ask questions instead of making statements
10. Listen

∆ What is the hardest part about listening for you?

_____
_____
_____
_____
_____

How can you make this more of a practice in your everyday communication?

_____
_____
_____
_____

What aspect of effective communication can you improve upon most?

_____
_____
_____
_____
_____
_____
_____

In what ways can you improve upon this?

_____
_____
_____
_____
_____
_____
_____

"It is well to remind ourselves that anxiety signifies a conflict, and so long as a conflict is going on, a constructive solution is possible".
–Rollo May

Dr.**Stem**

Unstoppable

Living A Free And Fearless Life

THE FREEDOM OF FORGIVENESS

One of the things that prevents us from communicating effectively and realizing our fullest potential is the lack of forgiveness. In some cases, people are so stubborn, they don't want to forgive because it keeps them in their comfort zone emotionally. Other people want to forgive, but they simply don't know how.

Forgiveness is the intentional and voluntary process by which a victim undergoes a change in attitude and/or releases negative emotions regarding an offense. The key phrases here are "change in attitude" and "release of negative emotion". If you want to get rid of the emotional strongholds we discussed earlier and communicate effectively, you must learn how to forgive. There's simply no way around it.

Holding onto negative emotions such as hurt, anger and bitterness can be extremely toxic. Not only do they distract you from focusing on the positive, they prevent you from moving forward. This is the complete opposite of being free. You must learn how to release the emotions that are keeping you bound so that you're not held captive by them. This isn't always easy, but it is absolutely necessary.

Holding on to an emotion that someone else has caused you allows you to continue to tell yourself that you are the victim and "they" are to blame. This gives the other person power over your destiny. It also gives you an excuse not to move forward.

Forgiving someone doesn't excuse what they did or take away from the fact that they hurt or disappointed you, it simply means that you no longer hold a grudge against them, and that you've made a conscious decision to release your ill-feelings and shift your attitude from one of malice to, essentially, one of compassion.

This doesn't mean you'll ever forget your experience with that person or how it made you feel; it means you decide not to allow that experience or emotion hold you bondage.

Forgiveness isn't limited to others. It's also important to learn to forgive yourself! At times, we can be so hard on ourselves that it's almost impossible to move forward. This makes it easy to fall into the trap of unworthiness and other emotional strongholds. Rather than playing the "blame game" with yourself, acknowledge where you fell short and identify ways you can improve on yourself. Don't stunt your growth by holding yourself hostage because you don't know how to let go!

Holding on to old baggage doesn't leave you room to accept or even acknowledge positive things in your life. It robs you of your focus and hinders you from experiencing the joy you deserve. The more "emotional waste" you eliminate, the healthier you'll become— emotionally, mentally, spiritually, and physically.

Furthermore, "emotional waste" contributes to stress. Stress is a major contributor to most major health complications, such as heart disease and stroke. It also results in a decline in mental health. Your mission is to be unstoppable and free. Don't allow emotional waste like unforgiveness to rob you of your health, peace of mind and purpose.

Self- Reflection
The Freedom Of Forgiveness

Forgiveness is an amazingly powerful gesture which has the power to:

1. Release freedom and happiness

2. To allow us to move forward without ever having to focus on the past.

When we fail to forgive, forgiveness has the power to:

1. Bind us and hold us captive

2. Cause hurt and pain.

Many people today find themselves on a leash. The links in the chain are anger, bitterness, resentment, and revenge. All these, however, come down to one thing—unforgiveness. Unforgiveness holds people hostage, and when they try to pull away, unforgiveness pulls them right back.

Unfortunately, it is easy to find yourself a prisoner of what others have done, and at times, something that you have done to yourself.

Forgiveness is a gift you give to yourself

Forgiveness does not mean approving a wrong or excusing an evil. Forgiveness is not necessarily the reconciliation of a relationship. The Greek word translated forgiveness literally means "to release." Forgiveness is your choice to release a person from an obligation for a wrong committed against you.

Δ Think of a time when you had a hard time forgiving someone. How did your inability to forgive impact you personally?

_____
_____
_____
_____
_____
_____
_____
_____
_____
_____
_____

∆ **Describe a time when you were able to forgive someone. How did it make you feel?**

_____
_____
_____
_____
_____
_____
_____

Did you see a difference in your attitude or perspective toward life?

_____
_____
_____
_____
_____
_____
_____

¡PATIENCE

One of the easiest ways to get discouraged is to lack patience. Being easily discouraged causes you to feel easily defeated. Patience is the capacity to accept, tolerate, delay, trouble, and suffering without getting angry or upset. It allows us to trust in the process without feeling discouraged when things don't go our way.

Sometimes, we get so easily discouraged because things aren't going our way that we become reactionary or begin operating out of desperation. The problem with forcing our own process or timing onto achieving our mission is that we often times get in the way. What you think might be "moving things along" might actually be setting you back.

Patience is a skill that requires the emotional competence we discussed earlier. It requires you to not only trust in the process, but trust in yourself and others who might be involved.

You have to trust that you've done your job in that you've done everything you were supposed to do to make the process work. You have to trust that those who are involved in the process are doing their due diligence. You have to believe that even when things don't happen on your timeline, it just wasn't the right timing.

If you haven't noticed, patience requires a great deal of trust. If there are people or things that are part of your process that have proven not to be trustworthy, despite your display of patience, you should certainly evaluate and readjust.

However, you must do this realizing that everything requires a process, and processes take time if they are to achieve any level of success.

Even when you recognize something didn't go according to plan because you fell short, have patience with yourself. Don't be so hard on yourself that you convince yourself you don't have what it takes or you're not good enough. It can be difficult to assess whether or not you have patience because you begin to wonder, "How long is too long?" No journey is too long, as long as you're learning and growing along the way.

Sometimes, when we feel the journey to achieving our mission is too long, we allow fear and doubt to creep in. Many people even bring their journey to a close because they fear they'll never get there. But, what they didn't know when they gave up was that success was right around the corner.

Being unstoppable means not letting anything get in your way, including how long it may take to get where you're going. One way to strengthen your patience is to appreciate the journey along the way. When you learn to appreciate every victory, no matter how small, patience becomes much easier.

You might be thinking, "Patience isn't the problem, I'm worried it's too late to start". It's never too late! If you have a passion and vision for something, start developing your roadmap now! You've heard that time waits for no one.

Well, your purpose is certainly waiting on you to come after it. And when you do, you must decide to be fearless. Free yourself of worry and have patience enough to commit to the process.

You don't have to be great to start, but you have to start to be great.

-Zig Ziglar

Self- Reflection
Patience

Like myself, I am sure, you have noticed that things don't always happen when you want them to. Sometimes, in between wanting something to happen and the actual happening, there seems to be a zillion years right?

That is when most people freak out and some lose it because of lack of patience. Life experience itself is the greatest teacher of patience.

I have learned that with patience you can...

o   do it better
o   enjoy the anticipation
o   get a better deal
o   make better connections
o   work authentically
o   take care
o   save more money
o   breathe
o   feel better faster
o   see good things happen
o   experience people being drawn to you
o   witness the best happen.

Signs of Impatience

How do you know when you're being impatient? You will probably experience one of more of the following:

o   Shallow breathing (short breaths).
o   Muscle tension.
o   Hand clenching/tightening.
o   Jiggling/restless feet.
o   Irritability/anger.
o   Anxiety/nervousness.
o   Rushing.
o   Snap/quick decisions.

Managing Impatience

When you feel impatient, it's important to get out of this frame of mind as quickly as possible. When you change what you are thinking, how you feel changes. Try these strategies:

- Take deep, slow breaths, and count to 10. Doing this helps slow your heart rate, relaxes your body, and distances you emotionally from the situation. If you're feeling really impatient, you might need to do a longer count, or do this several times.

- Impatience can cause you to tense your muscles involuntarily. So, consciously focus on relaxing your body. Again, take slow, deep breaths. Relax your muscles, from your toes up to the top of your head.

- Learn to manage your emotions. Remember, you have a choice in how you react in every situation. You can choose to be patient or choose not to be; it's all up to you.

- Force yourself to slow down. Make yourself speak and move more slowly. It will appear to others as if you're calm – and, by "acting" patient, you often "feel" more patient.

- Practice active listening and empathic listening. Make sure you give other people your full attention, and patiently plan your response to what they say.

- Remind yourself that your impatience rarely gets others to move faster – in fact, it can interfere with other people's ability to perform complex or highly-skilled work. All you're doing is creating more stress, which is completely unproductive.

- Try to talk yourself out of your impatient frame of mind. Remind yourself how silly it is that you're reacting this way. People often don't mind if a meeting is delayed, just as long as you let them know that you're running late in advance.

- If your impatience causes you to react in anger toward others, work on learning anger management to calm down.

- Some people become impatient because they're perfectionists. However, in addition to causing impatience, perfectionism can actually increase stress.

Remember that, although many people are naturally patient, the rest of us need to practice patience for it to become a habit. Becoming more patient won't happen overnight but do persist – it's so important!

Δ What is most difficult about practicing patience?

_____
_____
_____
_____
_____

Δ In what ways can you make patience a more tolerable part of your journey?

_____
_____
_____
_____
_____

"Character cannot be developed in ease and quiet. Only through experiences of trial and suffering can the soul be strengthened, vision cleared, ambition inspired and success achieved."
Helen Keller

Dr. **Stem**

Unstoppable

Living A Free And Fearless Life

¡GRATITUDE!

Appreciating your journey along the way is a very important factor of being free. When you fail to be appreciative of your journey, you become frustrated and bitter.

This will set you right back to the emotional strongholds you've worked so hard to overcome, regardless of how far your journey has taken you.

Recognize that every experience and every minute spent on your journey has provided you with something to be thankful for. It has allowed you to learn something new, grow to new heights, connect with people you otherwise would have never known, establish relationships, eliminate toxic relationships, recognize your own worth, and become a better you.

It's important to show appreciation for all that you've overcome and achieved, and show kindness in return. You should also be appreciative of the impact your journey has had on those around you, near and far.

Even if you haven't yet reached your destination, there is someone watching who you've inspired simply because you decided to take the first step toward achieving your vision. If you've already accomplished goals associated with your vision, think about the people you've impacted by doing so. If you've ever done anything on your journey that has positively impacted someone else, this is certainly something to be grateful for.

Learn to be grateful for every twist and turn, up and down, setback and comeback, because you never know who else you may have benefited along the way. After all, what good is achieving your life goal if you can't help someone else along the way?

Giving back is also a great way to show gratitude. Even if you don't yet have the means to give back financially, give back by showing appreciation. You can show your appreciation through kind words or providing those around you with opportunities they might not otherwise have had. Show appreciation through your kindness or by giving your time.

Show your appreciation through small gestures like public recognition, a smile or a hug. Simply sharing your knowledge with others is an act of gratitude. It's by doing things like these that make it evident to others that you have a heart of gratitude.

Your gratitude should be far-reaching. It should be felt by those who have supported you along the way, as well as complete strangers who might one day aspire to be where you are.

Gratitude might seem taxing, but the more appreciative you are of life, the easier it is. When you're really appreciative of life and all it has to offer, gratitude becomes like second nature.

Think about all of the amazing experiences you've had. Think about all the incredible people who have supported you along the way. Think about all the times your finances or health should have held you back but didn't.

Think about all the situations that could have caused you to fail or even cost you your life. Now, remind yourself that you're still here, and you're still working toward realizing your vision. It's for a reason! Be grateful for your reason and all of the potential reasons for your reason. This level of gratitude makes you unstoppable. This is what true freedom is all about!

Self- Reflection
Gratitude

Having gratitude helps us to enjoy life more. It can break through huge barriers and reduce our stress loads, give us more confidence and help us to meet our goals- no matter how big they may be. There is no doubt that being grateful goes a long way.

Figuring out how to be grateful in times of stress or when suffering from disappointment or sadness can be difficult. It is in those times that we should be reminded to turn to those things we are grateful for.

Often, we get caught up in a vicious cycle of "if only's". If only the job came through, then we would be grateful. If only the kids were better behaved, then we'd say "thanks". If only I could lose that extra ten pounds, get that guy to notice me, find a million dollars under my pillow…if only, if only, if only.

The problem with "if only" is that if and when the "if only" happens, we often just move onto the next thing without stopping to say "thanks". Or we focus so much on that hopeful if only, we forget to recognize all the other things we have in our lives to be thankful for.

There is so much each of us has to be grateful for. We just often forget to focus on the good at times. Gratitude can change our lives hugely. But first we need to take a look at where we are right now. Oprah Winfrey inspired me to start a gratitude journey which is really helpful when looking at everything that is going on in your life.

The following are sections you can use to write a gratitude journal.

Your finances - Do you feel you have enough? Do you think it's managed well? Do you feel a lack of money is affecting other areas?

Your work life - Do you enjoy your job? What parts do you like? Where is it taking you? Is there any part of you that is still wanting more from your job? In what way?

Your love life/ social life - Do you feel fulfilled and happy in this area? Do you feel loved and accepted for who you are? Do you have friends?

Your goals – Do you have goals? Do you have a sense of

where you are headed and do you know how to get there? DO you feel your goals are realistic for what you want to do and where you want to be?

Your physical life - Are you comfortable in your body? What parts are working well? What isn't doing so well? Are you filled with energy? Do you enjoy the foods you are eating?

Your home life and possessions? - Do you feel you have enough, or that you need more? Do you like the things you own? Have you got your favorite items that you treasure? What do you really long for? Is there anything?

1. Using the ideas I shared, make your list of the things you are grateful for.

2. Make another list of things you struggle to be grateful for, and compare them to the things you are already are thankful for.

Don't worry if the complaint list is a little long because when you work on changing the way you think, and start to fill your life with thankfulness, nothing will remain the same. You will begin to be grateful for those things one thought at a time.

Changing the way you see and think about any situation or feeling helps you to be grateful for big and small things, hurtful and painful things. You begin to acknowledge the silver lining.

Gratitude was the center of all that hype in The *Secret* and the *Law of Attraction*.

The movie and the book, THE SECRET expounds a simple life-formula. Think of it, thank the universe for it, and it happens. It talks about vibration. Gratitude brings about a vibration of joy, peace, happiness, anticipation and freedom to believe in anything being possible.

When you have the urge to debate why you should be grateful when you don't feel you have anything to be grateful about, change the way you are thinking to something positive. Find something to do that brings you to a better mood like e music, talking to friends, watching a movie.

Examples of things I am grateful for can help you with your list...

Things I Own

I am thankful for:

- Having shelter. I have a home to live in, a bed to sleep in and a place to put my things

- Having something to wear. I have something to keep me warm when the wind blows, and clothes I can wear on hot days. I can be covered and I have more than one outfit to choose from.

- I have shoes for my feet. I can cover them to protect them form sharp objects and to support my feet as I walk.
- Having the means to travel. I can use my car to get to places (or scooter, bike,) I have public transport available. I live in an age where it's easy to find a way to get somewhere fast if I need it.
- I have a computer to work on, play on and communicate with. Even if I have to borrow the use of one, I can use tools on it to find out information I can use.

My Liberty

I am thankful for:

- The fact I am alive.
- The chance to drink water from a tap and it's safe.
- The food I can choose to eat to fuel my body
- Being free, and imprisoned.
- Having the skills needed to read and to write.
- The opportunity to learn something new and life changing.
-

My Social Networks

I am thankful for:

- Myself. I'm who I am, and I accept myself.
- My loved ones. The special people in my life - those I've chosen to spend my life with, or give birth to.

- My parents who gave birth to me and the village that raised me.
- My friends and colleagues.
- My pets, for all their cuddles and our uncomplicated relationships

My Successes

I am thankful for:

- My innate talents.
- The skills I've learned
- My ability to make friends
- My job, or the way I support myself
- My interests, and the things I enjoy doing recreationally.
- My emotions.
- My choice to love others, and share my life with them

Significant Moments

I am thankful for:

- My move to Florida - Yeaaaa!
- Milestones in my life. Learning how to walk, to talk, to run, to laugh.
- My special days such as birthdays and anniversaries

- Memories. Times spent with loved ones.
- Holidays and time spent away from work
- Being able to order a takeout, coffee or having a meal out.
- Unexpected and pleasant surprises.

Life's Little Treasures

I am thankful for:
- Being able to feel the sun/wind/rain on my face.
- Going to the beach, or climbing a hill and looking out.
- Washing/drying on a windy day,
- Seeing a stranger smile at me.
- Watching snow fall.
- Taking my dog for a walk.
- Playing on playground equipment.
- Laughing.

Things I never expected

I am thankful for:
- The things I didn't get right the first time.
- The opportunities I didn't get the first time.
- The lovers that didn't work.

- The doors that closed on me when I wanted them open.
- The lessons I've learned though my experiences.

Use this list as a starting point and add any specifics you want. It's a good idea to put the list on the fridge, or somewhere you can see it to remind yourself to be thankful throughout the day. Soon, it will be second nature and you'll start to attract more good things to be thankful for, a lot more.

Thoughts Become Things

Δ What are you most grateful for throughout your journey to become fearless and successful?

_____

_____

_____

_____

Δ What are some ways that you can make showing gratitude a consistent practice?

_____

_____

_____

_____

"Everything will happen for you all of a sudden and you will be thankful you didn't give up. Blessings are coming. Believe that." - Jay Shetty

Dr. **Stem**

Unstoppable

Living A Free And Fearless Life

Helping Others To Succeed

Helping others to succeed is one of the best ways to give back and find freedom. You can find all the success in the world, but if no one else can benefit or learn from it, how meaningful is your success?

You don't have to be an expert to help someone else succeed in achieving their goals. The people surrounding you can benefit from learning about any part of journey, good or bad. Unfortunately, many people fear that helping someone else achieve their goals will somehow take away from their success. Not only is this a huge misconception, it is also one that is born out of fear.

Fear tells us we can't get ahead if we help someone else get ahead. However, this is complete nonsense! In fact, the more we help each other get ahead, the more we can learn from one another and help one another along. Remember, everyone has a unique purpose. This means, even if your goals are similar to someone else's, they will ultimately be realized in their own unique ways for their own unique purpose.

So, the notion that helping others will somehow prevent you from achieving success is null and void.

Helping others also provides valuable life lessons that you just can't obtain anywhere else. For example, helping others allows you to learn about the needs of others in a way that might inform your vision and goals, and ultimately, benefit you in the long run.

Another beautiful gift of helping others is that it allows you to learn more about yourself. Sometimes, it's not until we help someone else that we discover our own personal gifts and talents. Other times, it's through helping others that we learn more about our strengths and weaknesses, whether it's how we relate to others or how resilient we are in our quest to achieve our vision.

Helping others serves as a good reminder of how far we've come, and, at the same time, a refresher to help fuel us to keep going. Helping others also helps us to establish a sense of leadership. In fact, it is one of the best ways to build leadership skills.

What better way to learn how to lead effectively than by demonstrating you are able to support someone else? Whether you're providing advice or simply leading by example, real leaders think beyond themselves. They know that leadership extends beyond position or title. They realize, in order to maintain success, they must have others around them who are able to sustain their efforts and take the work they started to even higher heights.

Helping others also helps you to establish your legacy. Ask yourself, do you want to be remembered by what you achieved or by how what you achieved transformed lives? If your answer is the latter, you should definitely be helping others along the way.

There is a freedom in helping others because you know that you've imparted your knowledge, skills and support onto someone else. It is also confirmation that no part of your journey is in vain.

"Become the best in the world at what you do. Keep redefining what you do until this is true."

– Naval Ravikant

Self- Reflection
Helping Others To Succeed

It has taken me years to understand that without a shadow of doubt, the fastest way to achieve success is to first help others succeed. Successful people are always looking for opportunities to help others. Unsuccessful people are always asking, "What's in it for me?"

The fact is, our greatest successes in life often come through helping others to succeed, and without question, when you focus on helping others succeed, your eventual payoff will always be far greater than your investment.

In every moment we all have an opportunity to help others. The key is for you to feel good working with, and helping people in whatever capacity you can at home, work and in your community.

∆ How has helping others succeed made you more fearless?

_____
_____
_____
_____
_____
_____

∆ What more would you like to do to help others succeed that would also help you on your journey to live free and fearlessly?

_____
_____
_____
_____
_____
_____
_____

"The size of your success is measured by the strength of your desire, the size of your dream and how you handle disappointment along the way." - Robert Kiyosaki

Dr. **Stem**

Unstoppable

Living A Free And Fearless Life

Creating A Life Of Success

By now, you are ready to be free and live fearlessly so that you can live your best life. However, there are several steps you must take to make this journey to freedom successful. The first step if deciding to be fearless. Don't just play around with the idea; make the decision to be fearless and that nothing will stop you. Most importantly, once you make this decision, commit to it.

Start by choosing to be happy. This means choosing yourself. We're taught to be selfless and put ourselves last. However, putting yourself first is not a selfish act. It's important to take care of yourself so that you can care for those who mean most to you.

You will also need to take care of yourself so that you have the health and energy you need to accomplish the life you've envisioned for yourself. Take care of yourself, not because you're more important that anyone or anything else, but because you want to be able to support the people and goals in your life.

Walk away from anything that does not bring you happiness. If it steals your joy, it will distract from your goals. Decide that you deserve to be happy, and that you won't tolerate anything less. You may have heard it before, but happiness really is a choice.

Choosing to be happy doesn't mean that everything will always go your way; it means that you are in control of your emotions and your outlook on life. It means choosing to see the joy and opportunity in everything, despite what may come.

The next step is making room and making time. Stop making excuses about not having time to live the fearless life you deserve. You'll find yourself wasting more time making excuses than taking action. Make time by making room. We allow ourselves to become so inundated with things to do that we can't keep up with our own schedules. Have you ever stopped to look at what you cram into your day-to-day? What is your daily routine?

What things are you doing that are absolutely necessary? What things are you doing that are purely out of habit? Determine the things that are being done based on habit but are not benefitting you in any way, and eliminate them. For example, if you come home from work and watch two hour-long sitcoms on television three days a week, choose one that you like best and put the others on hold for a while by recording.

Now, you've reduced six hours worth of television during the week to three. This means you've essentially gained an extra three hours. Do you know what you can do with an extra three hours a week? You can make time to read books and articles about that thing you've been dreaming of doing. You can finally begin drafting that book or idea that's been floating around in your head.

This doesn't just apply to television. You can stop spending unnecessary time on the phone throughout the day. It's very easy to spend up to an hour on the phone every day talking about absolutely nothing. You simply extend your time by answering the phone because it's hard not to answer when someone calls. You have to learn to tell people you're not available to talk or set your phone to "do not disturb", even if it's only for one hour out of your day.

This does not make you selfish with your time, it makes you disciplined with your time. The same concept applies to social media, as well. There are countless other ways to make time. It's up to you to recognize what they are and reclaim your time.

It's also important to establish a strong support system. Identify those people around you who love and support you. These are the people who are patient with you, always willing to lend a helping hand, and constantly share words of encouragement. They esteem you every step of the way.

They don't have to be subject matter experts, just positive and uplifting. These can be family members, friends or members of church and support groups.

If you're able to find professional networks with a similar mission to what you want to achieve, this can be another great avenue for support. Many professional networks provide training, online webinars and shared learning. These networks also allow you to ask questions and exchange ideas along your journey.

You must also hold yourself accountable if you want to create a life of success. Don't just say you're going to live fearlessly and seek to accomplish your vision, hold yourself to it!

Put everything you want to accomplish in writing. Record what you've accomplished so that you can track your progress. Pay attention to where you fall short of accomplishing a goal and identify why. Did you fail to make enough time? Did you decide not to do it because you were afraid it wouldn't work? Doing this allows you to hold yourself accountable to being fearless.

It helps you to keep fear and excuses at bay and serves as a constant reminder that you are responsible for carrying out everything you've set out to achieve, not anything or anyone else.

In addition to recording what you've accomplished, you should also record what's working well and what's not so that you can reassess and reevaluate. No one is perfect, nor is any process. However, reassessing your roadmap to success on an ongoing basis allows you to readjust so that your process is more effective.

For example, your vehicle requires that you bring it in to be serviced after so many miles. This must be done, no matter the type of car or how long it's been around to ensure that the vehicle is operating at its top performance. This routine maintenance ensures that the vehicle is operating properly and prevents any dangerous malfunctions or breakdowns by identifying potential problems so that they are readily fixed.

Your vision and life goals are much more valuable than the car you drive, so why wouldn't you give it the routine assessment it deserves? You want a vehicle that is unstoppable. You should be unstoppable, too!
Equally important to holding yourself accountable is being consistent. Being successful is not for the faint at heart.

Consistency takes commitment. It will require you to show up, fully committed (sometimes more committed than the last time), over and over again. It means continuing to push forward, no matter how tired or defeated you may feel.

Even when things are going well, it means not slacking off. You have to remain consistent in taking the necessary steps to achieve your goals if you want to be successful. This includes your work ethic and your attitude.

You must also remain humble. Humility a modest view of your own importance that will allow you to focus on what really is important to your success and that of those around you. Be very careful not to start out on a mission to create a life of success just to make yourself feel of great importance. Remember, your success isn't just about you.

Humility is one of the most overlooked qualities of being successful because it is thought by some to be a sign of weakness.

However, humility is a sign of true character and leadership. Humility is acknowledging that you didn't get to where you are by your efforts alone but by the efforts of all of those who have supported you. Humility means not always wanting to take all of the credit, but credit others.

It also means taking ownership when things go wrong, rather than trying to place the blame somewhere else. Creating a life of success is within reach. All you need to do is make up in your mind that you want to be successful and begin thinking and acting like a success.

Deciding to be fearless is a success in itself. Many people set out to establish successful lives without taking the necessary steps to eliminate the fear that hinders them, often resulting in failure before they're even off to a good start. Creating a life of success requires that you be in tune with yourself, respectful of those around you and optimistic about what's ahead of you.

Self-Reflection
Creating A Life Of Success

There are many different ways to create a successful life, but the strategy that works best for you may depend on your view of success itself. We often think of it as doing well at work or earning a high salary.

While professional accomplishments can be one piece of the puzzle, it leaves out many other important areas of life. Family, romantic relationships, academics, and athletics are just a few areas where people may strive for success.

Individual definitions of success may vary, but many would define it as being fulfilled, happy, safe, healthy, and loved. It is the ability to reach your goals in life, whatever those goals may be.

So what can you do to boost your chances of achieving these things? What are some of the habits of successful people?

There is no single right way to be successful. What works for you might not work for someone else. There may not be a perfect combination of ingredients that can guarantee success, but there are some basic steps I have learned to follow that has improved my chances of being successful in life, love, work, and much more.

1. Build a Growth Mindset

Those who have a growth mindset, on the other hand took the time to build it. They believed that they could change, grow, and learn through effort.

People who believe that they are capable of growth are more likely to achieve success. When things get tough, they look for ways to improve their skills and keep working toward success.

Here are some suggestions on you can you do to build a growth mindset?

- **Believe that your efforts matter.** Rather than thinking your abilities are fixed or stuck, believe that effort and hard work can lead to meaningful growth.

- **Learn new skills.** When faced with a challenge, you benefit more looking for ways to develop the knowledge and skills you need to overcome and triumph.

- **View failures as learning experiences.** With a growth mindset you don't believe that failure is a reflection of your abilities. Instead, you view it as a valuable source of experience from which you can learn and improve upon. If something that doesn't work, then you try something a little different.

2 Improve Your Emotional Intelligence

When it comes to creating a successful life, intelligence has long been believed to be one factor contributing to success in different areas of life, but some experts now suggest that emotional intelligent may actually matter even more.

Emotional intelligence refers to the ability to understand not only your own emotions, but those of others as well.

Here are some suggestions to help improve your emotional intelligence:

- **Paying attention to your own emotions.** Focus on identifying what you are feeling and what is causing those feelings.

- **Managing your emotions.** Step back and try to view things with an impartial eye. Avoid bottling up or repressing your feelings but look for healthy and appropriate ways of dealing with what you are feeling.

- **Listening to others.** This not only involves hearing what they are saying, but also paying attention to nonverbal signals and body language.

3 Develop Mental Toughness

Mental toughness is the ability to maintain zeal or strength to continue trying even in the face of obstacles. People who possess this mental strength see challenges as opportunities. They also feel that they have control over their own destiny. They are confident in their abilities to succeed, and are committed to finishing what they start.

The good thing is, anyone can build on their mental toughness at any phase of their life. Here are some suggestions to help improve your mental toughness and increase your chances of being successful in life?

- **Believe in yourself.** Cut out the negative self-talk and look for ways to stay positive and self-encouraging.

- **Keeping trying.** Even when things seem impossible or setbacks keep holding you back, focus on ways that you can develop your skills and keep soldiering forward. One of the key habits of successful people is to always look at setbacks or failures as learning opportunities.

- **Set goals.** Mentally tough people know that in order to achieve, they need to start by having attainable goals. These goals are not necessarily easy to reach, but by having something to aim for, you will be better able to move forward and overcome obstacles.

- **Find support.** Doing things alone can be difficult, but having a strong support system can make things easier. Mentors, friends, co-workers, and family members can cheer you one when things get tough, and even offer advice and assistance that can help you improve your chances for success.

4. Strengthen Your Willpower

Willpower is the ability to learn to persist in the face of challenges. Wait for the rewards of your hard work. This can often be the key to success in life.

Here are some strategies you can use to improve your willpower:

- **Try distracting yourself.** For example, if you are trying to lose weight but are having a difficult time staying away from your favorite snacks, distracting yourself during your moments of weakness can be an effective way to avoid giving in to temptation.

- **Practice.** Willpower is something you can build, but it takes time and effort. Start by making small goals that require will power to achieve, such as avoiding sugary snacks. As you build your ability to use your will power to achieve such small goals, you may find that your willpower is also stronger when working on much larger goals.

5. Focus on Intrinsic Motivations

What is it that motivates you the most? Do you find that the promise of external rewards keeps you reaching for your goals, or is it the more personal, intrinsic motivators that keep you feeling inspired?

Intrinsic motivators are those motivations that have you doing things that you enjoy them, find them meaningful, or you enjoy seeing yourself do. Research has shown that while incentives can be a better predictor of some types of performance, intrinsic motivators tend to be better at predicting performance quality.

So what can you do to boost your sense of intrinsic motivation?

- **Challenge yourself.** People often find that pursuing a goal that is achievable, but not necessarily easy, is a great way to increase their motivation to succeed. Challenges can keep you interested in a task, improve your self-esteem, and offer feedback on areas you can improve on.

- **Stay curious.** Look for things that grab your attention and that you would like to learn more about.

- **Take control.** It can be difficult to stay intrinsically motivated to pursue a goal if you don't feel that you have any real influence over the outcome. Look for ways that you can take an active role.

Don't fear competition. There might be other people out there trying to reach the same goals as you, but this doesn't mean that you should give up. It gives you something to compare your efforts to, and can even help inspire you to keep doing better.

6. Encourage Yourself to Be of High Potential

If you are trying to learn how to be successful in life, consider what you can do to develop these key traits:

Conscientiousness: Conscientious people consider the effects of their actions. They also consider how other people will react and feel.

You can develop your consciousness trait by:

- Thinking about the consequences of actions
- Considering other people's perspectives

Accepting of Ambiguity: Life is full of situations that are not always clear. People with a great deal of potential for success are better able to accept this ambiguity. Rather than being rigid and inflexible, they are ready to adapt when the unexpected comes their way.

You can learn to accept ambiguity by:

- Challenging your perspectives and considering opinions and ideas other than your own
- Not fearing the unfamiliar
- Being willing to change
- Valuing diversity

Capable of Adjustment: In addition to being able to accept ambiguity, success is often centered around the ability to quickly adjust to change.

Some ways that you can nurture this ability to adjust:

- Try refrain from avoiding difficult situations and see them as opportunities to learn and grow rather than obstacles.

- See difficult situations as opportunities to help you adapt and recover faster.

- Be open to change. If you find yourself getting stressed out when plans or situations change, step back and look at ways to cope.

Courageous: If you want to know how to be successful in life, look at the characteristics of the world's most successful people. One thing you might quickly find is that they often all show great courage. They are willing to take risks, even in the face of potential failure.

So what can you do to improve your tolerance of risk?

- Utilize positive thinking.

- Utilize positive emotions to overcome fear.

- Look for ways to suppress negative emotions by focusing on more positive feelings.

Curiosity: People who are successful tend to be curious about the world around them. They are always eager to attain new knowledge and skills.

You can cultivate your sense of curiosity by:

- Taking and doing tasks that match with your interests or learning new ways of doing tasks to match your interest.

- You might find filing paperwork boring, for example, but looking for a more efficient way to categorize the information might play to your strengths as an organizer.

Competitiveness: Successful people are able to utilize competition to motivate, but avoid falling prey to jealousy.

You can develop a healthy sense of competition by:

- Focusing on your own improvements. Rather than worry about being the best at something, pay attention to your progress. Note how far you've come and things you can consider improving even further.

- Be happy when others succeed. Don't give into jealousy. Instead, focus on feeling genuinely glad when others do well and use to help them inspire you to be successful in your own life.

Δ What does creating a life of success look like for you?

_____

_____

_____

_____

_____

_____

_____

_____

_____

Δ What are some areas where you've struggled to create a life of success for yourself?

_____
_____
_____
_____
_____
_____
_____
_____

Δ What can you do to improve in these areas?

_____
_____
_____
_____
_____
_____
_____
_____

‼ Celebrate Small Success

Don't be afraid to celebrate your successes, even the small ones. You've worked hard and you did a great job. Learn to pat yourself on the back every once in a while. Celebrating your success doesn't make you self-absorbed. It simply allows you to slow down, take it in, and re-energize for the next step on your journey to success.

There is a difference between flaunting success and celebrating your accomplishments. If the intent of your celebration is to rub your success in someone's face or make them feel "lesser than", you're not celebrating, you're taunting. However, if your intention is to remind yourself of how awesome of a job you're doing and motivate yourself to keep moving forward, by all means, celebrate! Don't be boastful, be grateful. Be cheerful!

Small successes are important because they're often the ones that matter most. Sometimes, we get so caught up in trying to achieve our ultimate goal, that we miss all the little things worth celebrating along the way. For example, if your goal is to become healthier by losing 50 pounds within the next year, don't wait to celebrate after you've lost 50 pounds. Celebrate the small victories throughout the process that have positively impacted your life. Celebrate that you drink more water and feel more replenished throughout the day.

Celebrate that you're making healthier food choices, improving your overall health. Celebrate that you get a few more steps in a day and have more energy to spend with family and friends. Even though you may not have reached your goal of 50 pounds just yet, you are achieving so many important victories as you go. Celebrate at 10 pounds, then again at 20, and so on.

Celebrating small successes keeps you motivated because it helps to remind you that you are capable of winning and that you are one step closer to achieving your goal. This gives you hope and fuel to keep going. Don't be so modest that you can't celebrate yourself. Be proud of what you've accomplished.

You don't have to spend of lot of money to celebrate your successes. You just have to commit to acknowledging your successes in a way that makes you happy. You can give yourself some extra "me" time or treat yourself to your favorite dessert (a healthy choice in moderation, of course). Maybe you can pay a visit to your favorite restaurant for take out and give yourself a break from cooking for a day. Visit your favorite coffee shop or shopping store and give yourself a limit on what you can spend.

You can also celebrate your success by passing it forward to someone else. You ever notice that major food chains or department stores provide free food or merchandise when they're celebrating a huge anniversary, like 20 or 25 years?

This is in part a marketing move, but they also know that celebrating without including those who helped make them a success is important. So, as a way to say 'thank you', they pass on savings to you so that they can continue to be successful.

Again, don't go spending lots of money for every little success, but be sure to find ways to acknowledge your successes and all of the people and things that have contributed to it.

SELF-REFLECTION
CELEBRATE SMALL SUCCESS

When we make a small mistake, we almost always feel bad about it. But when we accomplish a small goal, we almost never feel good about it. Striving is good, but never being satisfied is bad. Is it possible to do both--aim for higher achievement while still taking time to enjoy the achievements you've attained? I believe it is. Here are some ways you can be on your way to celebrating your small successes.

1. Set small goals as well as big ones.

This applies to your life and business or career goals. I learned that achieving small goals and big goals can both be done if your mindset is right. You have the mindset that knows you can achieve the big goals with ease, just as you would with small goals.

2. Celebrate when you reach one of your small goals.

Whenever you hit one of your goals, no matter how small, stop for a while to enjoy the success.

3. Brag.

Share with others, as part of celebrating your achievements. Share on your social media to let the world know. Celebrating achieved moments will force you to take those achievements seriously and do more.

It will raise your profile, which is always a good thing.

Besides, the surest way to see that your accomplishments get the recognition they deserve is to begin by recognizing them yourself. Yeaaaaa!!!

4. Think back to where you started.

What did you hope to achieve? Maybe you've already met those goals, or maybe those goals have changed. Either way, always remember where and who you were when you started dreaming big or started launching your project goal.

Recognizing what you have overcome and where you started is a big energy and confidence booster.

5. Feel lucky.

You should feel lukcy because you are. How? Because you decide to be. It is a decision to feel lucky. So decide and know that you are lucky and voila, you are unstoppable.

6. Think beyond your career.

It will end someday, although most people do not like to think about that. (I certainly do.) I want to have time to relax, look back, mentor someone young, enjoy the proceeds of my hard work and. I also wish to attend events and celebrations of those that I have served and just enjoy life before my time is up.

When that day comes, will you look back on a time that you enjoyed as much as you could? Or will you just remember a collection of moments trying to get where you wanted to go next?

It's a choice each of us has to make, and I don't want to make the wrong one. So, each time I reach a goal I make sure that I stop long enough to savor the moment and celebrate.

What about you?

∆ Describe one or two small successes you've had on your journey to live fearlessly. Have you taken the time to celebrate these? If so, how?

_____

_____

_____

_____

_____

∆ What are some ways you can hold yourself accountable for celebrating your successes?

_____

_____

_____

_____

_____

_____

_____

_____

_____

"Having faith, beliefs, and convictions is a great thing, but your life is measured by the actions you take based upon them."

– Nick Vujicic

"Think of yourself as on the threshold of unparalleled success. A whole, clear, glorious life lies before you. Achieve! Achieve!"
Andrew Carnegie

Dr. **Stem**

Unstoppable

Living A Free And Fearless Life

Love Laugh And Live

A true test of how fearless you really are is your ability to live life to its fullest extent. If you are holding back in any area of your life, even your personal life, you are not living fearlessly. If you want to live life fully and freely, you must learn how to love, laugh, have fun and explore without allowing fear to hold you back.

Start by loving yourself. This goes back to self- worth. Learn how to value yourself and appreciate you for you. Love the way you think, love your body, love your personality, love your dreams and aspirations, love everything about you. Why? Because you're you, and there's no one else on the planet earth like you. If that's not worth loving, what is? It's also important to realize that it's impossible to fully love anyone else if you don't love yourself.

Loving yourself is not enough. You must also learn to love others. There is nothing more fulfilling than giving love away. In fact, love isn't love until you've given it away. Learn to love people through your words and actions. Give them words of encouragement, show up when they need you most, listen and seek to understand, show empathy, rather than judgement, and give mercy, rather than always holding grudges.

So many people are miserable because they do not know how to love other people. They are often selfish, bitter and cold because they are so afraid of giving love and being taken advantage of or not receiving it in return. But to live freely, you must live fearlessly and love openly.

Knowing how to love is only half the battle if you can't enjoy life. Learn not to always take yourself so seriously and laugh a little. It's ok! You've heard laughter is good for the soul. This is because it is a welcome distraction to our stress. It fills us with joy and connects us with people in a human way. Laughter is a form of happiness and hope. It's a sign that you're still alive and open to the thrill of life. Laughter is contagious, so spread it around as much as you can. Everyone can use a bit of laughter.

Did you know that laugher is also good for your health? Researchers from Vanderbilt University and all over the globe have found that laughter helps to decrease stress hormones and increases immune cells and infection-fighting antibodies. It also triggers the release of endorphins, which promote an overall sense of well-being and can even temporarily relieve pain. It burns a few calories, too.

When you love and laugh, you can live! Do things that you enjoy. Don't worry about how silly you might look or what others might think. You have one life to live, so live it to its fullest potential.

Be open to exploring new things and take on new risks. Stretch yourself to try something you've never tried before simply because you can. Most of all, have fun while doing it. Now that's living fearlessly!

> *"Success is to be measured not so much by the position that one has reached in life as by the obstacles which he has overcome."*
>
> -Booker T. Washington

Self-Reflection
Love, Laugh & Live

To me, Love, Laugh and Live is living life to the fullest. It means looking for the good and the positive in all people and situations as much as you can. Here are some tips to help empower you create a life of loving, laughing and living:

- Learn to listen and listen to learn.
- Learn from mistakes but let go of past "what-ifs."
- Laugh whenever you can, especially at yourself.
- Lift up others.
- Lead with grace.
- Lead with Hope
- Lose with faith.
- Lose with grace.
- Live with hope.
- Love.

Δ On a scale of 1 to 10, 10 being the highest and 1 being the lowest, how well would you say you live life to the fullest and why?

Δ What are some things you can do to love, laugh and live more?

"When your desires are strong enough you will appear to possess superhuman powers to achieve. Napoleon Hill"

Dr. **Stem**

Unstoppable

Living A Free And Fearless Life

Hope Peace And Joy

Now that you are ready to live fearlessly and be unstoppable in life, get ready for the hope, peace and joy that comes with it! True freedom is to live without hindrance or restraint. When you do this, your life will never be the same.

For starters, living fearlessly brings so much hope to your life. You constantly have something to look forward to because you have a vision and you're not afraid of failure. Just knowing that you have a chance at succeeding in life and an opportunity to make a difference along the way brings you new hope every day.

Hope allows you to see the glass half full, instead of half empty. It allows you to see the positive in things, rather than focusing only on the negative. It reminds you of your reason and gives you fuel to keep going.

The peace of mind that comes with living fearlessly is unmatched. When you walk in your purpose and decide not to let fear overshadow your vision, you have peace that you are living as you were intended to be.

There is a difference in the level of peace you experience when you're operating in your purpose compared to living with uncertainty.

When you decide to live fearlessly and walk in your purpose, you know there is a reason for everything that happens throughout your journey. When you're uncertain about whether you're on the right journey, you question every step, every turn, and even your own sense of direction. This is because you don't have a sense of purpose or direction, which leads to doubt and fear. Peace can only be found when you strip fear of its power and live with a purpose.

When you decide to live fearlessly, you also experience incredible joy. Knowing that you're moving toward something great and being confident that nothing can stop you gives you a sense of happiness that you simply cannot experience when you're living in fear. Living fearlessly makes you want to get up in the morning and makes you excited to start your day.

When you live fearlessly, you experience joy so powerful, that you can smile through the upsets because you know it's not the end for you. You even recognize that some of your setbacks are actually blessings in disguise because you were headed in the wrong direction or needed to pause and recognize something important that you would have otherwise missed.

Your joy and happiness is not only a delight for you, but for those around you. The same is true for your sense of peace. You'll find that other people will find comfort in you because you are not easily rattled and filled with positivity.

Finally, deciding to live fearlessly is absolutely freeing! The ability to walk in your purpose with no fear and be joyous about every part of your experience will make you feel as though you are walking on a cloud. It really does make you feel unstoppable. To be unstoppable is to be free.

Freedom allows you to keep moving forward, even when disappoints happen. This is because your sense of freedom won't allow anything to keep you bound. The true test of freedom is continuing to live freely and fearlessly, even when things get tough. If you regress back to your emotional strongholds the minute trouble shows up, you are not truly free.

It's up to you to choose freedom and live fearlessly. It's up to you to remind yourself that you are unstoppable, and you have all the tools you need to do anything you put your mind to. Why not now? Take control of your life and decide to be unstoppable today

Self-Reflection
Hope, Peace & Joy

A life of Hope, Peace and Joy is what we all strive for strive for in the end. Here are some points of encouragement to help you create a life filled with calm, peace and hope. along the way.

1. Thoughts and feelings become things

Remember How you feel about yourself is how you shape your reality. You can literally change the way you feel about someone orsomething and change your life in an instant.

2. You don't have to have all the answers

You do not need to know why all things happen in your life. Sometimes life just happens. Parents can only do the best they can, whatever they didn't do right, do it for yourself.

3. Be Creative

Life is about being creative; being free to be and do anything your heart desires. I am amazed at how many people live in their own prison. They literally live in miserable relationships, jobs, families and die slowly each day. This is your one life, live it creatively.

4. Be open to life and all it's great possibilities.

You are alive for a reason, be open to life and all that it has to offer. There is so much you can do and enjoy at every level. Make your days count in whatever way you choose to. Your life your choices are yours to make.

5. Embrace your life, your journey.

Everyone has a deeper story, something that they fantasize about doing if they could. What's your deeper story? What do you long for?

6. Understand your fears and know that you have control over them when they appear in your life.

7. As you read earlier, practice positive affirmations

8. Be open and willing to see things in a different way

9. Put yourself first.

Remember: If you can shape it in your mind, you will find it in your life.

Create vision boards and really start believing that you deserve to be happy in all areas of your life. Dreams do come true, they do.

Δ Describe a time when living fearlessly brought you hope, peace and joy. How did this impact your life?

_____
_____
_____
_____
_____
_____

Δ In what ways do you feel living fearlessly will increasingly bring hope, peace and joy into your life?

_____
_____
_____
_____
_____
_____

Some days you just have to create your own Sunshine

Dr. **Stem**

Unstoppable

Living A Free And Fearless Life

MOTIVATIONAL QUOTES
FOR BEING UNSTOPPABLE, FREE AND FEARLESS

- "Sometimes the bad things that happen in our lives put us directly on the path to the best things that will ever happen to us".

- "Life is the art of drawing without an eraser".

- "Remember it's just a bad day. Not a bad life".

- "Enjoy the little things in life. For one day you'll look back and realize they were the big things".

- "In three words I can sum up everything I've learned about life: it goes on." - Robert Frost

- "Challenges are what makes life interesting and overcoming them is what makes life meaningful."
  - Joshua J. Marine

- "Life does not get easier. You just get stronger".

- "Do not pray for an easy life. Pray for the strength to endure a difficult one." *- Bruce Lee*

- "Dream as if you'll live forever, live as if you'll die tomorrow".

- "Life begins when you step out of your comfort zone".

- "Don't say you don't have enough time. You have exactly the same number of hours per day that were given to Helen Keller, Pasteur, Michaelangelo, Mother Teresa, Leonardo da Vinci, Thomas Jefferson, and Albert Einstein". *–Jackson Brown Jr.*

- "All progress takes place outside of your comfort zone. *–Michael John Bobak*

- Our greatest fear should not be of failure, but of succeeding at things in life that don't really matter". *– Francis Chan*

- "Most of the important things in the world have been accomplished by people who have kept on trying when there seemed to be no help at all". –Dale Carnegie

- "Procrastination is the thief of time". *–Edward Young*

- "There is no secret to success. It is the result of preparation, hard work, and learning from failure". *– General Colin Powell.*

- "Perseverance is failing 19 times and succeeding the 20th". *–Julie Andrews*

- "So many of our dreams at first seem impossible, then they seem improbable, and then, when we summon the will, they soon become inevitable". **–Christopher Reeve**

- "There is no elevator to success. You have to take the stairs". **- Zig Ziglar**

- "When you get to the end of the rope, tie a knot and hang on". **–Franklin D Roosevelt**

- "The ultimate measure of a man is not where he stands in moments of comfort and convenience, but where he stands at times of challenge and controversy". **–Martin Luther King, Jnr**

- "Real difficulties can be overcome; it is only the imaginary ones that are unconquerable".
- **–Theodore N Vali**

- "Shoot for the moon. Even if you miss, you'll land among the stars". **–Les Brown**

- "Seventy percent of success in life is showing up". **– Woody Allen**

- "You've got to get up every morning with determination if you're going to go to bed with satisfaction". **–George Lorimer**

- "The important thing is not to stop questioning. Curiosity has its own reason for existence. One cannot help but be in awe when he contemplates the mysteries of eternity, of life, of the marvelous structure of reality. It is enough if one tries merely to comprehend a little of this mystery each day. Never lose a holy curiosity. ... Don't stop to marvel". –*Albert Einstein*

- "Your time is limited, so don't waste it living someone else's life". – *Steve Jobs*

- "Courage doesn't always roar. Sometimes courage is the quiet voice at the end of the day saying 'I will try again tomorrow'. –*Mary Anne Radmacher*

- "A successful man is one who can lay a firm foundation with the bricks others have thrown at him".
  – *David Brinkley*

- "Great things are not done by impulse, but by a series of small things brought together". –Vincent Van Gogh

- "You are never too old to set another goal or to dream a new dream". –*C.S Lewis*
-
- "Motivation is what gets you started. Habit is what keeps you going". –*Jim Ryun*

It's Time To Fly!

The journey has been long and painful at times. I now understand it is all worth it, as life prepares each of us for our time to fly like eagles and fulfill our purpose. My time is now.

To help you understand this journey of becoming unstoppable, I will encourage you by sharing with you the story of the butterfly.

Once a little boy was playing outdoors and found a fascinating caterpillar. He carefully picked it up and took it home to show his mother. He asked his mother if he could keep it, and she said he could if he would take good care of it.

The little boy got a large jar from his mother and put plants to eat, and a stick to climb on, in the jar. Every day he watched the caterpillar and brought it new plants to eat.

One day the caterpillar climbed up the stick and started acting strangely. The boy worriedly called his mother who came and understood that the caterpillar was creating a cocoon. The mother explained to the boy how the caterpillar was going to go through a metamorphosis and become a butterfly.

The little boy was thrilled to hear about the changes his caterpillar would go through. He watched every day, waiting for the butterfly to emerge. One day it happened, a small hole appeared in the cocoon and the butterfly started to struggle to come out.

At first the boy was excited, but soon he became concerned. The butterfly was struggling so hard to get out! It looked like it couldn't break free! It looked desperate! It looked like it was making no progress!

The boy was so concerned he decided to help. He ran to get scissors, and then walked back (because he had learned not to run with scissors...). He snipped the cocoon to make the hole bigger and the butterfly quickly emerged!

As the butterfly came out the boy was surprised. It had a swollen body and small, shriveled wings. He continued to watch the butterfly expecting that, at any moment, the wings would dry out, enlarge and expand to support the swollen body. He knew that in time the body would shrink and the butterfly's wings would expand.

    But neither happened!

The butterfly spent the rest of its life crawling around with a swollen body and shriveled wings.

    It never was able to fly...

As the boy tried to figure out what had gone wrong his mother took him to talk to a scientist from a local college. He learned that the butterfly was **SUPPOSED** to struggle. In fact, the butterfly's struggle to push its way through the tiny opening of the cocoon pushes the fluid out of its body and into its wings.

Without the struggle, the butterfly would never, ever fly. The boy's good intentions hurt the butterfly.

As you go through life may you always keep in mind that struggling is an important part of any growth experience. To maximize your potential you will have to embrace the struggles, failures, pains and know that everything works together for your very best life. The struggles cause you to develop your ability to fly, and the fantastic ability to be **UNSTOPPABLE.**

As A Life-Career and Business Coach, Parent and Teen Coach, my gift to you is stronger wings...

Be Encouraged

"I want to be looked back on as being very innovative, very trusted and ethical and ultimately making a big difference in the world."

-*Sergey Brin*

EPILOGUE

Many of you know that I am big on encouraging, motivating and inspiring others. I wanted to end this book with some words of encouragement. Life is truly too short to sit back and watch days and moments go by. So, in conclusion, here are some life lessons my 53 years of this life time have taught me.

- Every experience you will go through in life will make you stronger, no matter how painful or difficult it seems. There may be times along the way when you feel alone.

- There are always friends to be made and new adventures to discover. There are always friends and family members who respect you for who you are.

- During difficult times, remember there is a deeper strength and an amazing abundance of courage, determination and peace, within you. Draw from this, call on your faith to uphold you, and you will make it through this time and find your joy again. Hang in there.

- Always know that there is good in life. Make an effort every moment to distress yourself from your worries and concerns. How often do you walk barefoot in the sand, enjoy the pleasure140 of singing birds, enjoy returning a smile, or making someone smile. I enjoy encouraging others and making light the burdens they carry.

- Return a smile and realize life is a series of levels—cycles of ups and downs, some easy, some challenging.

- No matter how hard life gets, we all learn, we grow strong in faith, we mature in understanding. The difficult times are often the best teachers. I learned, yes, there is good in every person and situation.

- Be good, reach for the good, be strong, trusting, and never ever give up.

- The one thing you really have to do is keep believing in yourself. There will be times in life when things will not work out for you, when everything seems to fall apart. During these moments, it is important for you to keep a positive attitude about your life and where you are going. It does get better.

- Many a time, you will wonder if you are making the right choices. People will knowingly and unknowingly discourage or challenge you. Stay strong and motivated to rise and make your vision come true.

- Your vision, dreams and heart desires should always take precedence over anyone else's opinions.

- Remember tomorrow is always a new day, new moment to begin again and new opportunity to make a different decision. Begin it well and trust you will make it different than yesterday.

- Live your life one day at a time and walk your path one step at a time, with courage, faith and determination. Keep your head up, the universe, God has a way of making everything work out for your good.

- I live by the serenity prayer and share it with everyone I can. I even wrote my book " The Power of Prayer" based on the serenity prayer. God grant me the serenity to accept the things I cannot change, the courage to change the things I can and the wisdom to know the difference. Reinhold Niebuhr.

- Only you know what is best for you. You have to ultimately listen to your own voice, your own wants and follow your instincts. Family, friends mean well but they do not know you and will never know you, like you know you.

- Never let old mistakes or misfortunes hold you back, learn from them, forgive yourself, or others and move on.

- I have learned to be encouraged by my courage to overcome obstacles. It is amazing how much inner strength we all possess. Be empowered by the courage to follow your dreams. Learn something from all those you meet and admire.

- Believe in yourself. Follow your heart. You will make mistakes. Your heart will be broken. You will be disappointed. You will disappoint others, hurt others and also discourage others. Be true to the strength within you, pay attention to the new understanding, awareness and strength each moment and person teaches you.

- Be strong to see things through. Never Give Up. Always remember, you are a strong person with unique gifts, talents, love, support and abilities that will carry you through any difficult time or failure, so...

BE BOLD ANYWAY.

Let's Connect

Join Dr. Stem on Face Book Live on Tuesday evenings for discussions on topics discussed in this book and more.

Enroll in Teen Empowerment Webinars and online courses, and connect with other teenagers around the world for moral support, fun and encouragement. All online programs are on:
https://www.drstemmie.com/

Look out for the Parent & Teen Empowerment Conference or Workshop coming to your city, a city near you or at sea. Inquire at drstem14@gmail.com

REMEMBER

After reading this book, I look forward to hearing your story and how you were able to boldly make decisions that have changed your life for the better. Email me at drstem14@gmail.com

If you would like me to interview you on my radio show The DrStem Show

https://americaoutloud.com/show/the-drstem-show/

Email me at drstem@americaoutloud.com

Unstoppable

Living A Free And Fearless Life

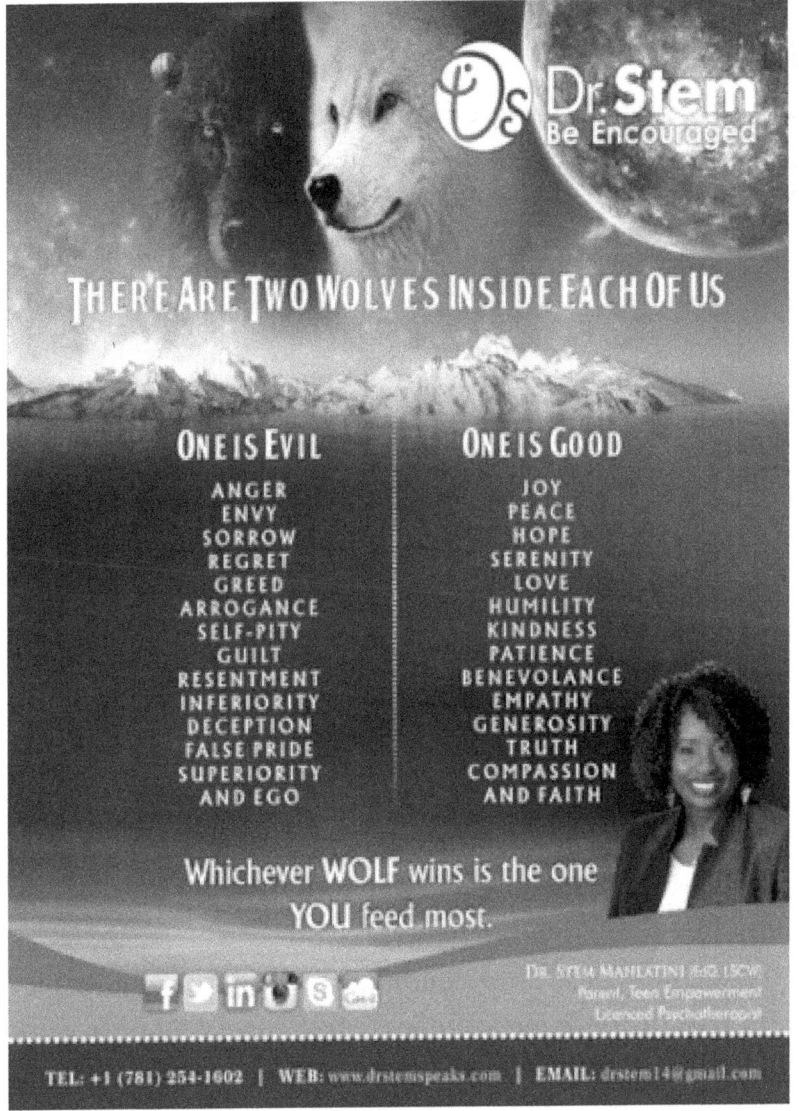

About The Author

Originally from Zimbabwe, Southern Africa, **Dr. Sithembile "Stem"Mahlatini** is president and owner of **Global Counseling & Coaching Services,** in Orlando, Florida, and she is also president and founder of Parent & Teen Empowerment Conference & Parent & Teen Empowerment Seminars.

She is a certified life-career coach, author, licensed psychotherapist and motivational/inspirational speaker. She resides in Orlando, Florida USA.

Dr. Stem's life's work is to inspire, motivate and educate others through her books, seminars, workshops, and Counseling and Coaching Services.

Drawing on her background as a licensed psychotherapist, life- career coach, speaker and author, she offers people practical advice on how to tap into their limitless power to change their lives, overcome roadblocks and aspire to be better than the circumstances that surround them.

Her life-long goal is to continue to empower and inspire teenagers, parents, and couples to be winners at home, work and business. Her motto is, "Each day is an opportunity to change your life and bring out the new you."

Dr. Mahlatini attended Nova Southeastern University where she earned a doctorate degree in education, specializing in organizational leadership. She is also a graduate of Boston University, where she earned a master's degree in social work, and she is licensed as a psychotherapist in Massachusetts and Florida.

She is a member of the Back Talk Toastmasters club, the Professional Woman Network, and the National Association of Social Workers.

Listen to DrStem weekly on The DrStem Show on https://americaoutloud.com/show/the-drstem-show/
Watch DrStem on The DrStem Show on Youtube for inspiration, encouragement and motivation through the interviews she conducts on the show, https://www.youtube.com/results?search_query=drstem+show

In addition to speaking and training, she counsels and coaches clients in her private practice offices in Altamonte Springs, Skype and telephonically. She serves clientele throughout the United States, Africa, the Caribbean, the United Kingdom, and Australia through one-on-one telephone coaching services.

Dr. Stem is available as a trainer and speaker for onsite trainings, groups, and one- on-one coaching for parents, teenagers, women and organizations. Consultations are conducted by telephone or on-site. Her programs include:

- Bridging the Gap Between Parents and Teenagers
- Pampering The "Princess Within"
- Overcoming Being All Things to All People
- Possibilities – Turning Dreams into Reality
- Free at Last – Setting Boundaries
- How to Deal with Toxic People
- 15 Strategies to Achieve Your Dream
- How to Live a Simpler Life
- Living a New Life of Confidence- Developing A Healthy Self Esteem
- Taking Charge of Your Life, Money and Family
- Change Your Thinking – Change Your Life
- The Rollercoaster Ride Is Over! Handling Emotions
- Handling Stress: Sink, Swim or Float & MoreBook

Dr. Stem Mahlatini as your next motivational/ inspirational speaker for your women's retreat, church, youth retreat, seminar, school assembly, or Business Management–Employee event.

Training, Individual and Group Life Coaching

Contact Dr. Stem Mahlatini at: PHONE: (781) 254-1602

Dr. Stem authored/co-authored the following titles:

1. Beyond the Tears-Bruised but Not Broken- Author Biography-A story of Hope & Encouragement
2. The Power of Prayer & Belief
3. It's Time to Shift -From Fear to Faith
4. Finding Your True Self
5. Emotional Wellness for Women vol. 1
6. Emotional Wellness for Women vol. II
7. Emotional Wellness for Women vol. III
8. The Baby Boomer's Handbook for Women
9. The Power of God
10. Celebration of Life-Inspiration for Women
11. How to Survive When Your Ship Is Sinking: Weathering Life's Storms
12. Beyond the Scars: Real Life Accounts for Women Who Overcame Adversity

13. Confident not Corky: Why self-esteem is Key to a Successful Life, Business and Career

14. Unstoppable: A woman's Guide to Self- confidence book and workbook.

15. Zero Limits: A Teenager's Guide to Life's choices

16. 471/2 Things to Say to Your Teenager and How to Say Them

17. 471/2 Things Teenagers Need to Know About Getting Along with Their Parents

18. CDC- Courage Determination Confidence: A Teenager's Handbook to Socially Acceptable Life Skills

19. 365 Daily Success & Motivation Doses for Teens

20. 50; A celebration of Life Lessons

21. Dose of Motivation & Encouragement for Teachers

22. Profits are Better than Wages: The key to Living Your Dreams

23. Finding your True Self – Bringing Clarity and Purpose to Your Life

24. Respect- Connecting with Disconnected Students: Seven Steps to Reach the Students You Teach

25. The Blessings of Being a Woman: Embracing Womanhood

26. Build Confidence, Achieve Success

27. Success within reach: reconditioning your paradigm

www.ingramcontent.com/pod-product-compliance
Lightning Source LLC
Chambersburg PA
CBHW052023070526
44584CB00016B/1880